# Wolf at the Door

*The World War II Antisubmarine
Battle for Hampton Roads*

# Wolf at the Door

*The World War II Antisubmarine
Battle for Hampton Roads, Virginia*

by James R. Powell and Alan B. Flanders

Brandylane Publishers, Inc.

Richmond, Virginia

❊ Brandylane Publishers, Inc.
1711 East Main Street, Suite 9, Richmond, VA 23223
(804) 644.3090 or (800) 553.6922
email: *brandy@crosslink.net*

*Library of Congress Cataloging-in-Publication Data*

Powell, James R., 1960-
 Wolf at the door : the World War II antisubmarine battle for Hampton
Roads / by James R. Powell and Alan B. Flanders.
 p. cm.
Includes bibliographical references and index.
 ISBN 1-883911-57-5
 1. World War, 1939-1945--Naval operations--Submarine. 2. Hampton
Roads Region (Va.)--History, Naval--20th century. 3. Operation
Drumbeat, 1942. 4. United States. Navy. Naval District, 5th--History--
20th century. 5. World War, 1939-1945--Campaigns--Atlantic Ocean. 6.
Atlantic Coast (North America)--History--20th century. 7. Coast defens-
es--United States--History--20th century. I. Flanders, Alan B. II. Title.

D783.P68 2004
940.54'516--dc22
2003020989

This book is dedicated to the memory of Dr. Stanley H. Powell, whose rich memories of World War II helped to inspire this book. It is also worthy of note that he served as a medical doctor to the citizens of Portsmouth, Virginia for sixty-two years before retiring.

*Wolf at the Door* is dedicated to the heroes who served in the U.S. Navy, Coast Guard, and Army, as well as civilians who helped to plan and implement the victorious Antisubmarine Warfare campaign against "the best men and machines the German Navy could muster."

# TABLE OF CONTENTS

# PREFACE

In *Wolf at the Door*, we return to a time during World War II when U-boats threatened the operations of the Fifth Naval District and nearly severed America's artery of supplies to England. The magnitude of this threat and how the Navy and the Army cooperated to bring security to the region and finally defeat to the U-boats is revealed. This volume complements other histories written on the battle of the Atlantic and the U-boat offensive along America's East Coast. But we place special emphasis on the American military's efforts to counter the German Navy's effort to eliminate Allied access to the Chesapeake Bay and Hampton Roads, and to obliterate all shipping in the Fifth Naval District.

We also hope that this research may dispel persistent rumors about enemy penetration into the Chesapeake Bay. Thus, in addition to challenging the personal stories of former U-boat officers, we examine newspaper accounts against the background of historical fact. For example, when a convoy did in fact strike mines left off Virginia Beach by *U-701*, the local newspapers erroneously reported that the ships were torpedoed. The papers failed to correct their mistake until long after the war was over, leaving some to continue believing that a close-in torpedo attack did occur.

Many of those who lived here during World War II have forgotten about the U-boat presence so close to home. Most people raised in this area after the war have never heard of the fighting just offshore, or, at best, have only heard rumors. It is partially for this reason that interest has grown recently to learn the truth.

It has become fashionable for some to criticize the Navy for waiting until after the U-boats were off the East Coast and sinking ships seemingly at will before implementing an effective defense. With regard to the U-boat successes off the East Coast, arguments now appear to make the Navy seem negligent, even callous. Such criticisms argue that the Navy could have easily and immediately established an effective defense of the entire East Coast the moment the threat was detected. However, nothing could be further from the truth.

Enormous preparation was needed. Essential military departments were required, personnel had to be selected and trained, and extremely scarce resources had to be obtained and deployed where they could be expected to do the most good. American public attention was riveted to events in the Pacific after Pearl Harbor. It is understandable that the first cry for action and revenge was aimed at Japan rather than Germany. Consequently, the daunting task of developing a strategy to deal with the U-boat threat was further hindered by popular will. Just how the American military broke this fixation and opened a second defensive front is the principal theme of this book.

The real heroes of this story are the thousands of men and women who served in the U.S. Navy, Coast Guard, and Army as well as their civilian counterparts who planned and implemented a successful ASW campaign against the best men and machines the German Navy could muster. Out of respect for all those involved in this effort, this story is told, and to their memory it is dedicated.

# ACKNOWLEDGEMENTS

*Wolf at the Door* began as a thesis by James R. Powell while earning his Master's Degree in history at Old Dominion University, Norfolk, Virginia. Naval historian Dr. Alan B. Flanders joined Powell to broaden the scope of the original outline to include interviews of participants from both Navies who played major roles in the conflict. From this effort, the following story of the development of United States Navy Antisubmarine Warfare Program (ASW) during World War II in the Fifth Naval District was developed. During their research, Powell and Flanders were able to locate American and German veterans and expert witnesses who developed the tactics and strategies that would finally determine who would control the East Coast of the United States at the beginning of World War II.

The authors were fortunate to locate three of the original five German U-boat captains who led the initial attacks on the United States during the critical first two years of the struggle, 1942 and 1943. Subsequently, they traveled to Germany and conducted extensive interviews with Reinhard Hardegen, Horst Degen, and Helmut Rathke. Much original information was obtained during these discussions covering such subjects as German preplanning, U.S. ASW intelligence operations, knowledge of the American coast, particularly the Fifth Naval District; and German U-boat tactics and strategies to avoid detection. Their memories about actual engagements against American air and surface forces are still remarkably sharp and offer an interesting perspective on the development of U.S. ASW efforts from its beginnings to the end of 1943 when the tide had at last turned against them.

The opening shots of this battle came during one of the darkest periods of United States history when German U-boats ravaged Allied shipping along the Atlantic coast just months after the devastating Japanese attack on Pearl Harbor. One of the most successful hunting grounds for these deadly, undersea marauders was in the waters of the Fifth Naval District. It was here in the home waters of the Atlantic Fleet along the shores of Delaware, Maryland, Virginia, and North Carolina that an organized antisubmarine effort was initiated by the United States Navy. How these efforts were planned and implemented is described by those who participated, when possible, and from primary sources when available.

This work complements other histories of antisubmarine warfare during World War II, which have not focused on the defenses established for the Fifth Naval District. The sacrifices and struggle by America's armed forces in defending the district deserve to be told.

The resources available in the library and archives of the Naval Historical Center in Washington, D.C. have been used extensively. Other sources include museums and archives in Virginia and in Germany, local historians, veterans of the war, and records in private collections. Whenever possible, first person accounts that could be substantiated by official documentation, rather than recollection alone, were used. Thus, one of the goals is to give the reader an "over-the-shoulder" perspective of the men and women who recognized the deadly strategy of Operation Drumbeat and finally developed a defense to ward off the "Wolf at the Door" of the Fifth Naval District.

We would like to thank the following people and institutions who contributed to this project: from Old Dominion University, Dr. Peter Stewart, Dr. Patrick Rollins, and Dr. Carl Boyd; from the Life-Saving Museum, Angus Murdock, retired Army Lieutenant Colonel Fielding Tyler, and Frank R. Shield; from the Hampton Roads Naval Museum, Ensign Edward Hayes; from the Operational Archives of the Naval Historical Center in Washington, D.C., archivist Kathy Lloyd; from the Casemate Museum, archivist David Johnson; also, retired Navy Captain Henry Clark, an expert on antisubmarine warfare training; Mavis R. Powell for aid in proof-reading, and Thomas H. Powell for assistance in producing the computer-generated charts herein; and Ms. Frauke Elbe, who served as translator during our initial correspondence with former German U-boat captains and later agreed to accompany us to Germany during our interviews with Reinhard Hardegen, Horst Degen, and Helmut Rathke.

Once again, I am most grateful to St. Edmund Hall, Oxford University, for providing overall support for this project. The undergraduate librarian, Ms. Deborah Hayward Eaton, is also acknowledged for once again allowing the author complete access to the Emden Naval History Collection. Without the continued support of St. Edmund Hall, the completion of this project would not have been as timely or as enjoyable as it was.

Finally, my wife Leslie Flanders, daughter Shannon, and son Nicholas, continue to serve as stalwart shipmates as my research and adventures in naval history continues.

# CHAPTER 1

## *THE FAVORABLE SITUATION*

"... Sooner or later, of course, these favorable conditions would gradually disappear. When our U-boats appeared in the western Atlantic, the Americans would strengthen their defenses, and these, with practical experience, would become progressively more effective. Ships would cease to sail independently and the convoy system would be introduced. It was, therefore, of primary importance to take full advantage of the favorable situation as quickly as possible and with all available forces, before the anticipated changes occurred."

Karl Doenitz
German Grand Admiral

During the early days of World War II, the United States was the major source of war material for England during its struggle for survival against Germany. Adolf Hitler understood that it was this support that enabled England to withstand his nation's staggering offensive. If this lifeline from America could be cut, or reduced to an insignificant level, England could be strangled and starved into submission, giving the Axis control over Western Europe.

Realizing this, the Germans unleashed elements of their powerful fleet of Unterseebooten, or U-boats, against both the transatlantic convoys and the source of these vital supplies, the East Coast of America. Soon after the Japanese delivered their devastating attack on Pearl Harbor, the German Navy began Operation Drumbeat, which brought five U-boats to the coast of Virginia, where they created havoc with shipping and alerted the local armed forces to the reality that the war had indeed come home.

Germany's Grand Admiral Karl Doenitz had asked the Naval High

Command for 10 Type IX U-boats but was only granted the use of six. The German navy was being very conservative with its U-boats as they only had ninety-one in operation. In December, 1941, one-third of these were in shipyards undergoing repairs with the remainder committed to operations in the North Atlantic, the Mediterranean, and off the African West Coast. In the end only five were sent to American home waters as the *U-128* was forced to remain in port because of mechanical problems. The five that did come to American waters were the *U-66*, commanded by KK Richard Zapp, *U-109*, commanded by KL Heinrich Bleichrodt, *U-123*, commanded by KK Reinhard Hardegan, *U-125*, commanded by KL Ulrich Folkers, and the *U-130*, commanded by KK Ernst Kols. Despite their small numbers, these U-boats proved formidable adversaries, attacking 24 Allied ships, of which 22 were sunk.

The coast of Virginia was listed second only to New York by the German high command as a primary target. At stake in Hampton Roads, Virginia, was a vital part of the nation's economy with such natural features as the mammoth Chesapeake Bay, numerous rivers, tributaries, and harbors. The region was also the home of the Naval Operating Base, Norfolk; the Norfolk Naval Shipyard, Portsmouth; and the Army's Fort Story at Cape Henry and Fort John Custis at Cape Charles. Prominent military installations on the nearby Virginia Peninsula included Fort Monroe and Fort Eustis. Hampton Roads, Virginia, was the heart of what was then called the Fifth Naval District. It occupied an area that included not only Virginia but parts of Maryland, West Virginia, and North Carolina. The district maintained jurisdiction 15 miles out to sea during wartime from its headquarters at the Norfolk Naval Station. After the war, all naval districts except the Naval District of Washington were abolished. Today, the function of these districts has been turned over to the naval station commanders. However, similar Naval districts will be reestablished should another major war occur.[1] (See Figure 1.)

Causing an untold loss of life, the U-boats were much more than just a nuisance; they were a destructive and lethal threat to the nation's war effort in addition to strangling Great Britain's supply lines.

The U-boat of choice to work these fertile waters was the Type VII, 704 of which were built in a number of variations including types A, B, C, D, etc., during the war. Weighing over 700 tons when surfaced and devoid of fuel, the basic Type VII measured 218 feet in length, 31.5 feet from keel to bridge, and 20 feet in the beam. Designed with a one-inch- thick pressure hull, it was capable of submerging to 100 meters or approximately 300 feet. Depending upon the skill of the crew, it could dive below the surface in 30 to 60 seconds. Typically, U-boats like these were manned by a crew of 44 men, including 4 officers.

Type VIIs carried two huge diesel engines that could propel them along the surface at approximately 17.5 knots while producing between 2,800 and 3,200 horsepower. Underwater, they were run by two electric motors that made a maximum of 7.6 knots from a 750-horsepower powerplant. The U-boat captains usually preferred to run well under the maximum speed as this prolonged the charge on their batteries. The faster they ran, the shorter their range on auxiliary power.

The armament on the U-boats was impressive. Usually, the Type VII U-boats carried fourteen 21-inch diameter torpedoes, fired from four tubes forward and one aft. They carried electric torpedoes, capable of 30 knots, and compressed-air-driven torpedoes, capable of 44 knots. This considerable arsenal was augmented by a powerful 88mm deck gun, a 20mm antiaircraft gun, and additional machine guns, which could be brought from below and mounted on deck. As the war progressed and air attacks became more frequent, the Germans de-emphasized the heavy deck gun and enlarged the bridge to accommodate more powerful antiaircraft machine guns.[3]

Another venerable U-boat deployed by the Germans was the Type IX, which was, like its counterparts, built in a variety of styles, including a special design to serve as a refueling tanker (milk cow) for other U-boats at sea. Whereas the Type VII displaced 760 tons, its typical Type IX counterpart displaced 1,120. The former had a range of 6,500 nautical miles with its 113-ton fuel capacity. The latter, however, had a range of 11,000 miles with its 208-ton fuel capacity. The IX C also had an edge on speed, with a maximum surface speed of 18.3 knots produced by two nine-cylinder Maschinenfabrik Augsburg-Nurnberg (MAN) engines, each capable of producing 2,170 horsepower. They also had two dynamotors rated at 493 horsepower, which were capable of propelling the ship at 7.46 knots while submerged, but were usually run at 4 knots to conserve the battery life. The Type IX C also carried better armament, with 18 to 22 torpedoes compared to the Type VII's 12 to 14. Furthermore, it had two stern torpedo tubes rather than the Type VII's one.

Despite her numerous advantages, the Type IX C was far less suited for combat than its equivalent in the Type VII series. Its greater size required at least 35 seconds for a crash dive—five seconds longer than the Type VII. These extra five seconds were crucial during an air attack by a B-24 Liberator bomber. The ship's larger size also accounted for its sluggishness and difficult handling while submerged. A candid criticism of the Type IX C was given by Doenitz himself when he said, "These boats are easier to

locate than the Type VIIs, more complicated and therefore more vulner-
able to depth charges and are more difficult to control when submerged."
(*Lone Wolf: The Life and Death of U-Boat Ace Werner Henke* by Timothy
P. Mulligan, London: Westport, Connecticut, 1993, Praeger Publishers)

Whatever the deficiencies of the various U-boat classes, building
defenses against them during the first years of combat proved to be an
enormous task that called for the joint resources of both the Navy and the
Army. After nearly 50 years the "lessons learned" from this early onslaught
would be remembered in February 1990 when Admiral "Bud" Edney, then
Vice Chief of Naval Operations and Supreme Allied Commander, Atlantic,
stated at the United States Naval Institute's anti-submarine warfare (ASW)
seminar that the submarine was the original "stealth" vehicle, and has always
been the toughest opponent on the high seas. He added that the German
U-boat campaign came very close to turning the tide in World War II. Since
then the United States Navy has made ASW its highest priority.[4]

# CHAPTER 2

## *ARRIVAL OF THE WOLF*

Before the United States officially entered World War II, it was clear to officials in Washington that the nation had to prepare for a war it had previously sought to avoid or in some cases even ignore. However, America's colossal economic power as well as its untapped military potential made it too great a threat for the Axis powers to leave intact. In August 1940, the United States opened what President Franklin Roosevelt called the "arsenal of democracy" by appropriating approximately $200 million for "War Measure" projects.

Virginia received its lion's share of these projects which included dredging operations in Hampton Roads, enlarging the Naval Air Station and Norfolk Naval Shipyard, and increasing general port facilities for handling ships plus building barracks, storehouses, and other buildings. Employment soared locally as a result. Workers moved to the areas around the military bases, many bringing their families. The population of cities such as Portsmouth, home of the Norfolk Naval Shipyard, increased dramatically. The housing industry boomed as large apartment complexes and residential sections sprang up. (NOTE: The maternal grandparents of co-author Powell were part of this migration; moving from North Carolina to Portsmouth, they were among the first to reside in the new Williams Court Apartments which were built for the new shipyard employees and their families.) For most Americans, this economic revival meant an end to the Great Depression.

This obvious increase in activity could not escape notice abroad. For England and the United Kingdom, it was a sign of hope that America was readying herself to join the war effort. For Germany and its allies, it was an obvious source of concern, especially as America was no longer truly "neutral." America did not hide its preference for the Allied powers through

5

the "Cash and Carry" and "Lend-Lease" programs as President Franklin Delano Roosevelt referred to the United States as the "Arsenal of Democracy." Time, money, and manpower, lots of it, were committed to making the military facilities in Virginia around the Chesapeake Bay indispensable producers of war ships, aircraft, and material. The government wanted to protect this investment should America be forced into war. However, for many of those working in the shipyard, the war was an ocean away in Europe, and although Virginia was a great strategic target, the threat of attack was slight with an enemy so far away.

Nevertheless, on 7 December 1941, after word of the attack on Pearl Harbor reached the East Coast, all Fifth Naval District Army forts went on alert, and at the naval facilities battle stations were manned while ships hurriedly prepared to head out to sea. Of concern was that Germany might launch a sneak attack of its own, perhaps conducted similarly to the Japanese attack, with the Naval Operating Base at Norfolk or any other facilities as their target.[5]

Eventually the excitement, anger, and outrage over the first days of the war subsided with the East Coast seemingly ignored by the Germans. Calm returned. However, the Germans had hardly forgotten the strategic importance of America's East Coast. As workers went to and from the shipyards now running night and day, Germans were likewise working on their U-boats and training their crews for future missions that would bring havoc to the very heart of the Fifth Naval District.

Even though no enemy aircraft attacked Hampton Roads, the Germans had another card to play, one that proved in the end far more deadly. Their strategy was to paralyze the Fifth Naval District and eventually bring it to its knees by a U-boat offensive.

According to the Fifth Naval District war records, the Germans had three strategic reasons for launching their U-boats against the American coast in 1942. First, each shipload of supplies kept from America would hurt the economy, war production, and, ultimately, flow of materials to England. Second, the U-boat threat would force America to divert warships from the North Atlantic coastal defense, thereby making the transatlantic convoys more vulnerable to attack. Third, the Germans knew from their own intelligence sources that America's East Coast was unprepared for and inexperienced in combating U-boats.[6] And indeed, the entire East Coast proved unready for the battle-tested U-boats. The Navy's first reaction against this threat was only a "bureaucratic" move. Navy officials decided the best method to defend the coastline was to organize it into one administrative unit called the Eastern Sea Frontier. This frontier was protected by the newly established Atlantic Fleet and the naval local defense forces. It was the Fleet's duty to keep the enemy away from the Frontier, and it also became the responsibility of the Local Defense Forces to protect coastal shipping.[7] The Fifth Naval District had only four vessels suitable for offensive action against U-boats in December 1941. More ships were eventually added, but the process was painstakingly slow. This delay gave the U-boats free reign early in the war. The Germans called this their "Happy Time."[8] Air patrols were also extremely limited. Army air patrols from Langley Field's 65th Observation Group, First Air Support Command, had only two flights daily of one plane each beginning on 18 December 1941. Assigned to such a vast area, the patrols had little chance of finding a U-boat, especially as they typically remained submerged during the day. Nevertheless, these few aircraft continued their flights hoping to find a U-boat on the surface replenishing its air supply or recharging its batteries.

These patrols had a vast area of ocean to survey within the Fifth Naval District. The chances of finding a U-boat in such an expanse of sea was remote, especially as they typically remained submerged during the day, surfacing at night to stalk allied merchant ships. Nevertheless, these aircraft continued their patrols hoping to find a U-boat on the surface replenishing its air supply or recharging its batteries or perhaps to catch one close enough to the surface that its outline could be made out. The numbers of these aircraft were gradually increased by the latter part of 1942 along with improved offensive capabilities such as airborne radar.[9]

Lacking effective knowledge and control of merchant ship schedules, the limited Navy and Army patrols were incapable of effectively protecting the merchantmen, who, unaware of any danger, often sailed with their navigation lights burning. In addition, the coastline was not yet blacked out, which silhouetted the merchant ships, making them easy targets. This illumination also furnished arriving U-boats with precise landfalls. Both Virginia and Maryland pilot boats were lit with running lights, giving U-boat navigators an excellent advantage by which to target American and Allied ships. Not only were limited coastal convoys not in operation, but in the beginning of the battle, there were not enough escort vessels available to even consider convoying.[10]

Without coastal convoys, merchant ships presented easier targets for the U-boats. Escort ships were not then available, as all were committed to transatlantic convoy duty. Like so many lost sheep wandering out of the herd, independent merchantmen sailed heedlessly into the crosshairs of the waiting "wolf packs." Needless to say, both Navy and Coast Guard patrols were anxious to begin their ASW missions, but trying to get underway often proved a daunting task.

Frederick G. Swink, a Norfolk, Virginia, attorney, joined the United States Coast Guard in 1942 and subsequently was commissioned as a lieutenant, junior grade, when his unit was added to the United States Navy picket patrol in the Fifth Naval District. Reflecting on those terrible days as commanding officer of three United States Coast Guard patrol ships, the USS *Calypso, Dione,* and *Thetis,* he remembers the helplessness of the moment.

"In 1942, we had no escorts for those ships. They traveled singly and got knocked off five or six a night down there (Hatteras). People in Norfolk and Virginia Beach did not know about the severity of the sinkings, but people in Hatteras knew about them. On the Outer Banks, they had more and more oil, bodies, and debris coming ashore.[11]

"On patrol in Hatteras we would see ships on fire. But it seemed we would see them only at night. What the German submarines did was to lay on the bottom during the day and come up at night and attack on the surface. They had a beautiful target with the lighted shore.[12]

"Admiral Andrews was begging for escorts and Admiral King wanted escorts reserved only for transatlantic convoys. Admiral King had none available, but he felt the north Atlantic was most important. We knew what we needed, and Admiral Andrews knew, but he couldn't get more. I don't think Admiral King really had much of a feel for it. There were approximately 500 ships sunk along this coast between January and probably June (1942)," Swink recalled.[13]

In addition, there was the ongoing crisis in the Pacific theater, where Admiral Chester Nimitz needed every available vessel to contend with rapid Japanese advances. There were simply not enough ships to go around. On a single day in January 1942, the Germans, with little fear of retaliation, were able to attack 14 ships, 10 in the Fifth Naval District alone. A large number of these attacks occurred in sight of Cape Hatteras, North Carolina, and the Virginia Capes.[14]

Linwood Hudgins, former commanding officer of the 190-foot USS *Orchid*, a buoy tender that operated from the United States Coast Guard's buoy yard in Portsmouth, Virginia, remembers in detail what it was like to come across a U-boat victim, realizing the logistical limitations his ship and those like him had in attempting rescue. Despite her name, *Orchid* bristled with armament, including a 3-inch 50-caliber machine gun on the forecastle head and two antiaircraft guns on top of the captain's quarters. She also carried four more anti-aircraft guns on the after deck house and depth charge racks on port and starboard. Had she an encounter with a U-boat, no doubt it would have been an interesting one.

"I never actually saw a U-boat, but I did see the results of what they did in 1941 and 1942," recalled Hudgins. "I saw one (SS *Tiger*) hit just off Cape Henry in 1941. It was night and I saw the flash! We didn't go after her right then because we knew someone was taking care of her. We had a radio, but we were ordered to remain silent. We operated independently of the Navy as well. It was the Navy's job to take care of things like that. The only time I had involvement in rescuing something is when I got orders from Coast Guard Headquarters.[15]

"Your message would be brief—'SOS, SOS, latitude and longitude—proceed and assist.' And yes, you could hear the 'boom, boom.' They would also send me up and down to Elizabeth City by PBY (patrol airplane) to count the masts and smokestacks, and see how many buoys I had to take down there to mark the wrecks."[16]

During one incident, Hudgins had the *Orchid* about 75 miles east of Cape Hatteras when he received an "SOS." He remembers that by the time he reached Wimble Shoal, it was just daylight when he discovered "half a lifeboat, broken hatches, everything you could imagine from a ship that had been blown up. We could see things like that drifting all day. The weather was terrible. With a good southeast wind, it was rainy, misty, foggy—turn a light on and you couldn't see anything."[17]   Hudgins contradicts much official documentation that American warships and merchant vessels were still running with their navigation lights on.

"Nobody had any running lights. Everything was blacked out. We even had blackout switches on the door aboard *Orchid* so if you opened the door to go in from the deck, the light would go out. It was really dangerous running without lights because you could have a collision any time.[18]

"At any rate, as I followed all that debris, every once in a while, I would get a position on two lifeboats. I followed them all the way up to the Delaware breakwater. I learned later that they were Norwegian sailors and that they had rigged sails on their lifeboats and were heading north as fast as I was. I never did see them.[19]

"By the time we got up here, we were running short of fuel, food and water. We had been out a long time and we were short of everything. Then the engineer came up to me and told me the boiler had a bad leak and we were using extra water. I sent a message back to headquarters concerning our situation and they answered back, 'Continue to search!'"[20]

Soon after that, Captain Hudgins learned of the general condition of his power plant. "The engineer came up to the bridge and said, 'Unless we get fresh water in the boiler within 24 hours, I am going to put salt water in the boiler!' I sent a coded message and told them that we were certain to ruin our boilers if we continued the search. They radioed back, 'Discontinue search.' We learned later that afternoon that a destroyer had picked up the two lifeboats."[21] Captain Hudgins went on to say that he received a "proper dressing down" for not pursuing the rescue mission, but all was apparently forgiven once he produced his chief engineer's report. Apparently the continued strain on the *Orchid's* engines and the unrelenting search for survivors at sea was a condition shared by most patrol boats and ships during the first two years of war in the Fifth Naval District.

According to Captain Hudgins, *Orchid* never had the great fortune of finding any American or Allied survivors at sea. Once, however, he did come across an enemy corpse, which caused an inexplicable reaction by U.S. Navy officials.

"I picked up a German officer, I don't remember his name or anything about him. I carried him to the section base at Morehead, North Carolina. But we had contrary orders—not to pick them up." When asked what command the German sailor might have come from, Hudgins replied, "From a sunk U-boat no doubt [probably from the *U-85* commanded by Captain Eberhard Greger, sunk at about the same time Hudgins was operating just east of Cape Hatteras in 1942]. But then they told us not to bring any more dead bodies—that order came from the Navy!"[22]

When asked why the Navy would issue such an order, Hudgins could not offer an explanation. "We laid him out on the deck. We didn't bother to search him. No one touched him except to get him on board with grappling hooks."[23] From that point Hudgins explained that one of their most important missions other than tending channel buoys was to mark the exact location of sunken American and Allied merchant ships, which unfortunately kept them quite busy.

# CHAPTER 3

## *ON THE PROWL*

Long before Germany declared war on America, 11 December 1941, Grand Admiral Karl Doenitz, the man in command of Hitler's impressive submarine fleet, was fully aware of America's inexperience with U-boats. He knew that in time of war with the United States, this weakness would be only temporary and therefore had to be exploited to the fullest while it lasted. Realizing America's vast industrial capability to develop air and sea defenses and implement coastal convoys, Doenitz asked for liberal use of Germany's U-boat forces, including a daring deployment off America's East Coast. Hitler, however, denied permission for U-boats to sail into the Western Atlantic before the declaration of war. When war was declared against the United States, he restricted the number of U-boats, fearing an Allied invasion of occupied Norway.

Ironically, the German admiralty failed to prepare its deploying officers with basic intelligence about America's East Coast in general. Three surviving U-boat captains agreed that proper preplanning sessions were inadequate. In fact, Captain Reinhard Hardegan, one of the German Navy's most successful commanders, said, "It was the same way I made a patrol to Africa, to Freetown, and the patrol to Freetown was the same distance to New York. It was normal, it was like every patrol. I was just told to fuel the boat as much as I can. Fuel, petrol and all these things were then added. But I didn't know I was going to the coast of the United States before."[24]

According to Hardegan, German U-boat captains received their destination orders while underway. "I went off to Lorient. When I passed a designated longitude on 27 December, I remember quite sure, I opened the sealed orders and I knew for the first time that I had to go to the United States.[25]

"You see, when I was with the five commanders of Operation Drumbeat, Admiral Doenitz didn't say anything about the United States. But I

11

thought it must be the United States because I had a big boat, a Type-IX E (*U-boat 123*, which had a greater range than the Type VII), and fueling full was critical for the distance. So I knew we were at war with the United States and I only had to look on the chart and I could see—I can go to the coast, and I can go back, and then I will still have enough fuel to operate for ten or twelve days. So we hoped it was the United States, but Admiral Doenitz didn't say anything."[26]

Hardegan also recalled that his group, the first to sail for the United States, had no charts of the American coastline. However, he still cherishes a weathered booklet containing tourist maps and narrative descriptions of the United States. "Fortunately," admitted Hardegan, "I remembered that I had my old student tourist guide, and I used it to navigate along the coast."[27]

Captain Horst Degan (*U-701*), who also participated in the second wave of the attack along the East Coast, had little information beyond Hardegan's and agreed with his assessment of their lack of preparation. "I did not receive a briefing for the specific tour. I only got the point of destination—where to go, where to wait, where to stay for ships."[28]

Apparently there was some rivalry between U-boat commanders. Degan stated that, "One fellow captain came back just the day when I started going out there and that was Captain Schnee. He was out there in Operation Drumbeat and coming home from a very successful mission. I didn't know him personally. That afternoon I asked him, 'Couldn't you tell me anything about that area? What is up there? How is it?' He ignored me, thinking I was apprehensive about the mission. I was very angry about that!'"[29]

When told that his destination would be the Chesapeake Bay, Degen recalled that it came as a surprise. "I must be honest on that. I never heard of the Chesapeake Bay before. To me it was just another cape on the coastline. But when I got orders to go there, I had to get the sea chart and find where Chesapeake Bay was since it was the entrance to Washington, wasn't it? For us the most known area was the Atlantic together with the United Kingdom-England."[30]

Captain Hellmut Rathke (*U-352*), also a veteran of the second wave, underscored the German Navy's failure to thoroughly prepare its commanders for the American coast. "No, nothing at all," he began, "we had no briefing about the coast and not even information about our behavior as prisoners of war."[31]

Regardless of their inadequate planning, by January 1942 Doenitz finally got an extremely limited version of the massive offensive he argued for: Operation *Paukenschlag* (Roll of the Drums) against the United States. It began on 18 January with the sinking of two cargo ships and a tanker.

With only five submarines on station, a cargo ship was attacked every eight hours along the East Coast.[32] These results gave Doenitz a strong argument for more U-boats to deploy in a second attack planned for that March.[33]

In the first seven months of the operation, the tides grew heavy with the corpses of dead sailors when 585 ships, totaling more than three million gross tons of shipping, were sunk off the East Coast.[34] (There is a complete list in Appendix A of all ships attacked in the Fifth Naval District during the war.)

During these early months of the German offensive, U-boats typically attacked on the surface with either their torpedoes or deck guns. By the spring of 1942, however, the defenses along the East Coast improved as both Navy and Coast Guard vessels gained experience in using radar, sonar, and visual U-boat sightings to pinpoint and attack the marauders. According to Captain Hardegan, United States Navy leadership failed to take advantage of existing technology and intelligence from Great Britain to prepare for the U-boat onslaught." Admiral King had at his disposal 25 destroyers and he did nothing with them. In other words, in a way, his inaction saved my life! Also, to make matters worse, Admiral King apparently did not like the British, because he ignored all the information about us that they gave him. We did not know it yet, but they had cracked our naval cipher, 'Ultra,' and he did not use that information against us either. Because they could have read our mail, and didn't use the destroyers available to them, we thought maybe there is some kind of treaty and so on. But when we arrived at the coast, and if he had deployed the destroyers, we would have lost five submarines. That would have been considered normal. So we were totally astonished. There was nothing—no blackout—no dimming! We thought the Americans have been stupid. We had been at war for years with Great Britain, and I thought the British would tell their allies, the United States, how to war against submarines. And they did! But (Admiral) King did nothing. We heard later that a British captain had been sent to the United States to set up a special 'war' room against our submarines, tracking and so forth, before 1942, and nothing! And all the houses there were full of light and all the motorcars had their lights on as well. It was like in peacetime!"[35]

Although Virginia Governor Colgate Darden had ordered a blackout by March, 1942, Hardegan recalled that even during his second patrol, almost a year later, he found only a marginal attempt at preparedness. "Many houses along the coastline were still fully lit. Some lighthouses were dimmed though. Also, a lot of the ships were blacked out or darkened. But not all! There were also more airplanes and blimps. In other words, there was a little bit more effort, but only 10 percent of what I was used to off the coast of Great Britain. There it was incredible for us."[36]

During Hardegan's second patrol he sailed close to the coast where the waters are shallow, denying himself the safety of deep water in case of enemy attack. Despite the shallow water, affording less than 20 meters, Hardegan daringly ran his ship on the surface, confident that there was little chance of being detected or attacked. "While on the conning tower, I used my binoculars. When I was off the coast of Manhattan, I saw the city lights while we cruised along the lower bay. Despite later reports that I saw people dancing on the rooftop of the Hotel Astoria, that was impossible to see from a submarine. Even though I did see the lights of Long and Coney Island and the houses and motor cars, I did not see the Empire State Building despite what the American press claimed."[37]

Hardegan's luck did not last during his second patrol. His *U-123* was forced home for extensive repairs after an attack by the USS *Dahlgren*. Despite having his ship severely damaged he still refers to the tactics employed by the Americans as "amateurish.[38]

"Maybe the commander was a midshipman or a cadet," recalled Hardegan," because he had no idea how to attack a U-boat. He threw five depth charges. And we were at the time submerged 23 or 24 meters. We lost fuel, we lost our air pressure. We discovered later that we lost one section of our deck planks."[39]

However, despite Hardegan's initial condemnation of the *Dahlgren's* commanding officer, he grudgingly admitted that his ship was in grave danger of being sunk during the incident. "The destroyer came over us three or four times and we wondered about abandoning the boat. It is very difficult to leave a boat when a destroyer is coming because in the moment when we got out if he dropped depth charges our lungs will burst. We will be dead, all of us, because of the concussion and so on.[40]

"And so we waited. Then he tried once more. I was at my hatch cover and opened it a little bit and got some water down my neck. I turned it a quarter turn tighter. And then I waited a little more — 'blub, blub, blub' came, and nothing! And then he went off![41]

"Then we got an accurate damage report. Both of our diesel engines were disabled. Then the engineer added that only one of our electrical engines was functional. After arriving at periscope depth, I looked and saw that the *Dahlgren* was still in the vicinity. We went down to 50 meters and went around. The whole day we worked on repairs and the whole next day and night we heard ships going hither and thither. The *Dahlgren* always looked for where our air and fuel came and they thought the submarine was sunk, that it was destroyed. After the war I read the report of the captain of the *Dahlgren* and he said he sunk a submarine. He made a mistake. He should have waited for the white cap of the captain to appear on the surface. And so I escaped, I came back to France for repairs and so I am sitting here today."[42]

When asked how German U-boats during this period failed to intercept the largest transatlantic fleet that formed at Hampton Roads and other staging areas along the East Coast for Operation Torch and the liberation of French North Africa, 24 October, 1942, Hardegan had no answer. Either the U-boats were too busy elsewhere, the secrecy of the operation held, or the convoy simply escaped unscathed by luck.

Adjusting to America's growing skill, the Germans added mines to their arsenal.

One of the most successful U-boat mining operations of the war was carried out in Fifth Naval District waters by *U-701*. The captain of the *U-701*, Horst Degen, brought his Type VII U-boat out of port in Brest, France, on 19 May 1942, after completing general repairs. As part of Germany's second wave of attacks on the U.S. coast, it arrived over the Atlantic shelf on 11 June 1942.[43] Degen recalled, "Since my submarine was delayed at Brest for servicing, my original mission of taking agents was given to another U-boat. Rather than taking agents, I would be taking fifteen mines instead to the Chesapeake Bay.[44]

"I didn't think of any American antisubmarine measures. I just went there and thought, 'Well, let's see how they react! No reaction!' I must honestly say I didn't expect any American antisubmarine efforts."[45]

In an earlier memoir Degen described his approach to the American coastline while running on one engine at five knots to preserve fuel. "Day by day we came nearer to the American coast, we went slow but steady without any excitement, the spirit on board was good. The crew had good food and good entertainment by records being played in the wireless room over loudspeakers throughout the whole ship and when we were approaching the American coast there was also the U.S. radio stations giving us the latest news and musical programs not knowing whom they were entertaining.[46]

"We reckoned to be on the spot on 13 June 1942 which was 'General MacArthur's Day' as they had announced on the radio days ago. So let it be MacArthur's Day that we dedicate our presence by means of 15 magnetic mines. Full speed ahead towards the Chesapeake Bay! There were no airplanes and no Coast Guard cutters as the *U-701* drew nearer and nearer to the shore. Unmolested even by day we went on, no crash-diving needed.[47]

"We went up to the shore off Virginia and saw lighted cars along the beach. By night, we didn't dive because it was too shallow. We couldn't observe traffic where the ships came because it was too shallow. So I had to go right away to where the ships would come."[48]

Carrying three mines in each of its five torpedo tubes, with an additional nine torpedoes in storage, *U-701* approached the entrance of the Chesapeake Bay.[49] Degen described the extreme care and precision he used in deploying the mines. In order to lay the mines for the greatest possible effect, he wanted to observe the exact routes of the outgoing and incoming ships. To do this, he settled the *U-701* on the bottom in a mere 36 feet of water, bringing "the upper edge of our boat ... only a little under the surface."[50] Bottoming the ship in this way late in the evening of 11 June, Degen was able to observe the shipping the following day at periscope depth. Degen and his crew were justifiably worried that they might be spotted and captured intact, which would have been a bonanza of information for the United States. Degen commented, "One could as well have put her in an aquarium for easily catching her!"[51]

With their observations complete, the crew was able to plot the main Hampton Roads shipping channel with great accuracy on their charts. Safely submerged, they waited for perfect operational conditions. It was after midnight, 13 June, when the U-boat surfaced and entered the sea lanes. With a new moon, which gave no light to betray them, Degen took time to marvel at the illuminated lighthouses at Cape Henry and Cape Charles. As their course carried them toward Cape Henry along Virginia Beach, Degen could not believe the preponderance of lights. "It was a breath-taking adventure to see even cars and persons and lighted houses," he recalled.[52]

Once they headed north in the shipping channel and had Cape Charles along their port, they were soon in position to lay mines. Suddenly, in stark contrast to the bright coastline, an armed trawler with lights blacked out appeared in the channel on patrol. Anxious moments passed as the ship approached until it slowly changed course, missing the *U-701*.

At exactly 0130 Degen's crew went into action. As the *U-701* zigzagged in the channel under the power of her diesels, a mine was dropped every minute. Their mission was nearly half over when the same patrol trawler turned back into the channel, and once again began an approach. Degen remembered shutting down their diesel engines, choking off their characteristic diesel sound, and switching to the quieter electric motors.

"Suddenly, we saw a dark ship. It was the only thing on the horizon at that moment. They must have been careful. They put their lights out at night on the vessel.[53]

"But Cape Henry and Cape Charles were lighted—with beacons. I got my bearings from there. But then I noticed my diesels' noises were too strong, too loud, so I turned to my electric engines, so as not to disturb this lonesome patrol boat or trawler. If the captain of that boat is still alive, he could still be angry at not seeing me. But I don't blame him."[54]

Missing them again, the trawler passed by completely ignorant of the proceedings. Almost like they had rehearsed it, the *U-701* sneaked in behind the trawler's stern and followed it while they finished dropping their mines. By approximately 0200 the deed was done. Degen said, "We had a feeling that the mines were laid just on the right position since the trawler had shown us where she was guarding and which way we should not trespass."[55]

Their mission complete, the *U-701* stole away. "Now that our torpedo tubes were empty," recalled Degen, "we hurried to load the reserve torpedoes we had inside the boat, four in the stern where the enlisted men were quartered and one under the gangway between the electric engines for the stern engines. This reloading was done within about two hours during our march being submerged. Everybody was happy to get rid of those big 'cigars' having been stowed in two layers between the sailors' beds keeping the front room most uncomfortable. Now that the four front torpedoes were pushed into the shooting tubes the sailors were able to rig up a table and sit down for the meals."[56] Submerging the following day, they made little headway with their slow electric motors. Early in the evening, the order was given to surface and run on their diesels. "It went without saying," Degen added, "that after having dropped the mines the raid was to be continued by getting ready for hunting enemy ships with our torpedoes. In fact a radio message from our base in France reached us: '*U-701* was to go southward to Cape Hatteras and its vicinity!'"[57]

Degen readied his ship for what he hoped would be continued success for his mission. "Shortly after midnight," Degen continued, "we began with preparations for taking in the two outer torpedoes which were stowed in two pressure-tight tubes outside the ship's hull right below the gangway deck. This was an operation that took all the skill of our torpedo and sailor personnel. It is hard work and if a crew is not well trained for the job one should better not take those two torpedoes inside. But we had done the job before and needed the torpedoes badly enough since by carrying mines we already had five torpedoes fewer than other U-boats. So the equipment for loading the stored torpedoes was erected; the front outer-tube was opened, the torpedo was pulled out and was brought before the front-loading hatch. The ship must go slow and be kept on a course that does not give too much rolling to prevent the water from rushing into the ship through the open hatch. The torpedo was lowered into the front torpedo room and swiftly the hatch was closed behind."[58]

With the bow loading completed they were now ready to begin loading the stern torpedo. But, as Degen recounted, this nearly proved disastrous, straining the crew's nerves close to the breaking point. "This time things did not go as smooth as they did the first time. Something jammed and it took about an hour to get the rig all right again. It was a hell of a time because it began to dawn, this was no work to be done during the day as airplanes and enemy ships could get at us by surprise. And for the time the stern-hatch was open we could not think of diving. We would have been a dead duck if somebody had come to see us on the surface with open hatches, tangled ropes and a dozen men on deck!! But we pulled through and were able to submerge at last when the sun rose in the east! Now we had our torpedoes inside and were ready to meet enemy ships and attack them! It took us till noon to get everything inside the boat shipshape again. A look through the periscope told us that no ship was in the vicinity, nor could we see any airplanes on the horizon. So, in order to get to Cape Hatteras we blew the tanks, came to the surface for a quick march to our destination point."[59]

They proceeded at full speed down the coast, where Degen observed what he thought were several prime targets for his newly installed torpedoes. However, his hopes for several easy kills were soon dashed. "I found wrecked ships sticking out of the water. At night I observed them. There was a big steamer but it didn't seem to move at all. It was wrecked, sitting on the bottom with the funnels, the masts sticking out of the water. And this made me angry about my fellow Captain Schnee for not answering my questions. If I had known that these fellows were first down there and they had told me, I wouldn't have had all this trouble observing and pursuing dead ships."[60]

Even though this effort was not successful, his mines on the other hand would prove to be spectacularly successful. As his U-boat slipped away from the Chesapeake Bay, the 60-hour timers on the mines were clicking away. If deployment was completed at 0200 on the morning of 13 June, as stated by Horst Degen, the mines would have armed themselves at approximately 1400 on 15 June. If so, they were armed a little over three hours when they claimed their first victim.

A bright, pleasant day at Virginia Beach on June 15 attracted a large crowd of beachgoers. Late in the afternoon, Convoy KN-109 was visible offshore approaching Cape Henry and moving at five and a half knots. Preparing to enter Chesapeake Bay, the double column convoy of 12 ships began to form into a single file by Buoy 2CB. This display of large ships must have been an impressive sight from the beach. *U-701*'s trap was now set.

Suddenly the unmistakable sound of an explosion drew every eye seaward. At 1704, the fifth ship in the column, the 11,615-gross-ton American tanker, SS *Robert C. Tuttle*, laden with 142,700 barrels of crude oil, struck a mine along the starboard side of the bow, stopping her dead in the water.

*U-701*'s trap was sprung. One crewman, Rubin Redwine, second assistant engineer, was killed immediately. Witnesses and survivors recall that the ship's bow plunged downward to a depth of 54 feet of water, causing the stern to rise completely out of the water. Fortunately, the other 46 crewman got away successfully. Miraculously, the ship, although partially sunk, would later be salvaged along with 72,000 barrels of oil.[61]

Crowds of horrified onlookers gathered along the beach and pointed in the direction of what at first sounded like the dull rumble of thunder. Suddenly the MV *Esso Augusta*, along with other ships in the convoy, began to zigzag, fearing a U-boat attack. In the panic, *Esso Augusta*, an 11,237-gross- ton tanker, turned right into the path of disaster. Laden with 119,000 barrels of diesel oil, the unlucky ship found a second mine close astern on its starboard quarter. Unlike the SS *Robert C. Tuttle*, she did not sink, but was heavily damaged. While her crew concentrated on damage control, *Esso Augusta* was later towed by three tugs into Hampton Roads. Again, miraculously, only one crewman was hurt in a fall caused by the explosion.[62]

During the confusion from the explosions, crew members and beach-goers together felt certain the convoy was being ambushed by German submarines. Freeing themselves from momentary paralysis, the convoy's escort ships entered the fray. Almost immediately, the destroyer USS *Bainbridge* thought it made a sound contact with a U-boat! But given the number of wrecks already scattered across their chart, they could not be certain. Regardless, in the excitement of the moment, crewmen dropped two patterns of depth charges set for 50 feet. Following a second, equally dubious contact, eight more depth charges were dropped. Even though the depth charges found no U-boat, proof that enemy mines were in the channel was quickly forthcoming. After the eighth depth charge detonated, an unexpected ninth, more powerful explosion lifted the stern of the *Bainbridge* out of the water, forcing her to cut engines and assess damage.

A fourth act in *U-701*'s deadly drama still awaited the stunned audience on shore. The 500-gross-ton British armed trawler HMS *Kingston Ceylonite* entered the channel, escorting the SS *Delisle*, which was being towed by the USS *Warbler*. (Formerly the World War I-vintage Minesweeper No. 53, she was reclassified after private service in September 1941 as the salvage vessel USS *Warbler* (ARS-11), whereupon she took on duties towing disabled vessels and escorting coastwise convoys). At approximately 1915, the *Ceylonite* struck a mine. The first blast was followed by a second, most likely from the ship's magazine. Originating from the starboard side amidships, the explosions ripped her into two sections just forward of the bridge. Panic-stricken, the surviving crew members abandoned ship as the forward section listed to starboard and sank while the aft section floundered on an even keel. Only 15 of the 32-man crew survived; seven required medical treatment at the Portsmouth Naval Hospital, Portsmouth, Virginia, and the Marine Hospital in Norfolk.[63] Despite the severity of the damage and the carnage that resulted, there was no panic along the shore, nor in the nearby population centers, that the area might soon be under attack as it was still popularly held that the war was being fought on the opposite side of the Atlantic.

After these disasters, the port was ordered closed to all further traffic. Minesweeping resumed in earnest the next morning, 16 June, with a total of 13 ships deployed. During a complete sweep of the suspected area, three more mines were detonated near Buoy 2CB at the entrance of the Chesapeake Bay. An investigation later conducted by the Naval Inspector General concluded that the minesweeping operation was "unsatisfactory." It was also concluded that the six participating sweepers from the Mine Warfare School were "unready for sweeping operations," and that coordination was poor, which rendered the operation ineffective. Due apparently to a combination of confusion and human error, the sweepers failed to discover the remaining mines.

Following the "all clear" from the Navy, based more on wishful thinking than fact, Convoy KS-511, which had remained outside the bay during the minesweeping, proceeded with caution into the channel on the morning of 17 June 1942.[64] Tenth in the single column convoy was the 7,117-ton American collier, SS *Santore*, which carried a cargo of 11,095 tons of coal. At 0745, having passed Buoy 2CB, the *Santore* struck a mine that exploded amidships on her port side. The blast reportedly hurled coal 40 to 50 feet into the air. Even though the ship immediately began to capsize, most of the men were able to abandon ship leaving only three dead out of a 46-member crew. The Navy determined that the ship was unsalvageable and placed warning buoys over her location to warn mariners of the potential hazard. The *Santore* soon became a familiar monument to *U-701*'s mining success as she settled on her port beam with approximately three feet of her starboard beam visible above the water.[65]

All told, 11 mines were accounted for, including those struck by ships, set off by depth charges, or captured.[66] If the official analysis that a total of 15 mines was laid is correct, 4 must have drifted, or "walked," as described by the U.S. Navy, out of the channel, and have never been found.

Inspired by the success of this mission, the Germans tried a repeat performance. However, the *U-49*, which had arrived in the area on 10 September 1942, would not have the same luck as her predecessor. Even though the Germans laid 12 mines successfully off the Virginia Capes during the evening of 12 September 1942, they soon discovered that things had changed. This time the mines were not "discovered" by a passing convoy, but instead uncovered during a routine sweep of the channel near Buoy 2CB two days after they were set. The port was again immediately closed while the minesweepers continued their search. When their mission was completed, seven mines had been found and exploded, without further damage to shipping. The remaining five mines apparently "walked" without incident.[67]

Only after the war did the Allies learn from German records that this deadly drama was played out a third and fourth time. On 30 July 1943, the *U-566* reportedly laid 12 mines, which were undiscovered and produced no results whatsoever. The next day, the *U-230* supposedly laid 8 mines. They too went undetected.[68] Herbert A. Werner, the executive officer on the *U-230* under the command of Captain Paul Siegmann, recounted their purported mine laying operation within the Chesapeake Bay, in his published memoir, *Iron Coffins*. (For a full account of this unverified event, please see APPENDIX D.)

There is no evidence, however, to lend credence to his claim. If his account is true, he certainly defied the odds, because in July 1943, regular mine sweeps were conducted in the swept channels and certainly at least one of the mines should have been snagged. Furthermore, Werner described how he arrived between Cape Henry and Cape Charles and entered the Chesapeake Bay itself, where he said they could see the lights of Norfolk as they laid their mines. As the defenses were fully primed at this time, the U-boat would have passed over a U.S. Navy minefield, hydrophones, and a magnetic loop. It also would have had to avoid the 24-hour coastal lookout observers as well as the patrol craft.

The successes of *U-boats 123* and *701* are understandable due to the unprepared state of defenses at that time. After two years of war, with many lessons painfully learned, a lot had changed by July 1943 when Werner's *U-230* was supposed to have reached Virginia. Although a mining operation could have been done, at least some indication of its presence would have been noted by Allied reconnaissance. Assigned a mission that was nearly impossible by that time, Werner could have simply told his superiors what they wanted to hear "for the record."

During the spring of 1942, Italian submarines also announced their presence. On 24 April 1942, while sailing just 250 miles east of Cape Hatteras, the 7,340-gross-ton British freighter SS *Empire Drum* made a tragic contact with what was positively identified as a Settembrini-class Italian submarine. At 1745 Eastern Time, a torpedo ripped into her port side, and within seconds her cargo of 1,270 tons of explosives blasted a giant hole in her sides at the number one hold. Fortunately, the crew was able to abandon ship in an orderly fashion just a half-minute before a second torpedo tore into their ship. As the crew rowed from their dying ship, she disappeared, bow downward, into the sea. Then to the surprise of the survivors, the submarine, described later as having green hull paint and an unusually tall conning tower, surfaced and neared the lifeboats.

Four members of the submarine crew, dressed in Italian navy uniforms, hailed their victims in Italian. Realizing that they could not understand, one officer broke into English to get the name and tonnage of the sunken ship. Without further incident, the crew disappeared below and the submarine slipped away. Even though Italian submarine attacks were rare, they were nonetheless effective, like the 2 June 1942 sinking of the 6,827-gross-ton Norwegian tanker MV *Muldanger*. Despite these spectacular successes, the Italian submarine forces remained concentrated in the Mediterranean as a defensive force.

At any rate, the potential of German U-boat minelaying had been firmly established with the success of Degen's *U-701*, even though others were not able to follow her destructive path.

# CHAPTER 4

## *CALL TO ARMS*

Before the war, military planners in the Fifth Naval District understood that their area would be a "high priority" target. The Navy knew before the war that even a minimal defense of the region would be difficult and that defenses already in place were far from adequate, particularly against a U-boat offensive.

Fortunately, some early consideration had been given to coordinating the U.S. Army ashore with the Navy forces afloat. The Army, which originally had the primary task of repelling any invasion by the enemy with its heavily armed fortifications and ground forces (infantry), was ordered to work with the Navy in repelling any enemy U-boat offensive; this was a new and unfamiliar role for the Army. Working together under the dictates of a doctrine known as the "Joint Action of the Army and Navy (FTP 155)," they both sought to prevent any enemy intrusion.[69]

For the Navy, the preliminary weapon against the U-boats along the coast was the Local Defense Force, established in each district by Navy Basic War Plan Rainbow #1 (WPL-42), issued in September 1939. Rainbow #1 also established the Naval Coastal Force for protection of the entire North Atlantic Frontier. As the Navy had assumed command of the Coast Guard under a directive from the President, the Local Defense Forces included not just Naval vessels, but also those of the Coast Guard and its lightship service. Virginia pilots were also inducted into the Coast Guard during the crisis with the issuance of Coast Guard Memorandum CGR-057 to all district Coast Guard headquarters. Paragraph 1 of this memorandum read: "The reports on pilotage approved by the Secretary of the Navy on 27 November 1942, having been previously approved by those government agencies concerned with pilotage and accepted by all the state pilot associations are enclosed. The responsibility for the control of all pilotage in the United States now rests with the Coast Guard." Paragraph 2 added: "It is intended that each association of state-licensed pilots operate as a group of temporary members of the Coast Guard Reserve with the present president of that group acting for the duration as the senior Coast Guard Officer attached and who will be responsible directly to the District Coast Guard Officer for the efficient operation of that pilot group."[70] Thus, the burdensome weight of defending the coast fell to these combined forces.

Following America's entry into the war, the Navy immediately went to Basic War Plan Rainbow #5 (WPL-46), issued in May 1941. This plan put the defenses into a wartime mode as it set forth goals and tasks for the Navy and assigned duties. As a result of Rainbow #5, the Local Defense Force in the Fifth Naval District found that they were now officially expected to keep the harbors secure, keep mines out of the channels, patrol the coast, and protect shipping.[71]

Admiral Ernest J. King, Commander in Chief of the United States Fleet (later appointed Chief of Naval Operations), and Rear Admiral Adolphus Andrews, Commander of the Eastern Sea Frontier, were the initial architects of this plan. Now the defense perimeter extended out to sea along the entire eastern coast of United States. It was organized as one territory under one command to streamline operations and strengthen critical concerns such as antisubmarine warfare (ASW).[72] In the Fifth Naval District, the primary naval officer was the Commandant. This post was held by four men during the war: Rear Admiral Joseph K. Taussig, from 30 September 1938 to 16 June 1941; Rear Admiral Manley H. Simons, from 16 June 1941 to 31 May 1943; Rear Admiral Robert F. Leary, from 31 May 1943 to 30 October 1943; and Rear Admiral David M. Le Breten, from 30 October 1943 through the close of the war. The commandant needed assistance in managing the numerous and complex tasks involved in administering the Fifth Naval District. Consequently, the post of Assistant Commandant was created in June 1942, with Captain Russell S. Crenshaw taking command on 18 June 1942 and serving in this capacity until the end of hostilities[73] (see Figure 2).

With little regard to quality or condition, the commandant took over three 125-foot Coast Guard cutters, two Coast Guard tugs, and one 165-foot Coast Guard cutter, plus other small cutters, buoy tenders, and motor boats.[74] In many regards it resembled a "Dunkirk-style Fleet" more than a ready fighting force.

Under Rainbow #5, the commandant was also expected to secure "vessels from other sources," but few of these were available. The commandant was also expected to purchase privately owned vessels. Only a few, however, could be found that were large and sturdy enough for deployment, and these were usually classified as "unavailable" due to the owners' refusal to sell. The forces expected to be raised under Rainbow #5 were simply unobtainable. Out of the 19 vessels expected under "vessels from other sources," only one was finally acquired. All the other vessels procured needed new equipment such as modern radar and sonar. Although the Coast Guard ships were closest to meeting basic standards, they too were in need of repairs. It was hardly a surprise that the defenses mustered at the start of the war fell far below even the most modest expectation.[75]

Against the odds, the commandants never gave up seeking more local ships, or badgering Admirals King and Andrews to recognize their plight. Of course the Navy's top management was aware of the situation, but they were in the difficult position of fighting a global war, and even the emergency needs of the Fifth Naval District could not drown out the continuous cries for more immediate help in the Pacific. For the commandants though, anything was better than coming up empty handed, and occasionally persistence paid off. For example, when Commandant Simons endorsed a recommendation for 52 additional ships in October 1942, which was basically just another plea, Vice Admiral Andrews gave in, perhaps just to placate him for awhile, by relinquishing 10 additional patrol craft on a graduated basis.[76]

Additional vessels were also supplied by the British. In late March 1942, four 83-foot armed trawlers arrived in Norfolk. These were quickly put into service, with two operational by 31 March.[77] Through continued acquisitions of what amounted to two dozen British armed trawlers, patrols were gradually increased in the Eastern Sea Frontier.

In recognition that the Virginia coast was now a major target, President Franklin Roosevelt established the Chesapeake-Norfolk Defensive Sea Area in 1941. Now that it was a designated military zone, both Army and Navy forces were directed to coordinate their forces against the enemy. The Army heavy artillery provided long-range firepower extending to the limits of the designated area. On 15 July 1941, the Chief of Naval Operations set up the following boundaries:

> A line running from the southernmost point of Cape
> Charles, Virginia, to Cape Charles Lighthouse on Smith
> Island, thence on a bearing 130_ True to the Seaward
> limit of U.S. territorial waters to the parallel of Latitude
> 36_51'15" North and thence west meeting the shore at
> the U.S. Coast Guard Station, Virginia Beach, Virginia.[78]

On 11 December 1941, active control of this Defensive Sea Area began with the installation of an outer guard ship stationed approximately four miles east of Cape Henry. A "Notice to Mariners" issued on 24 December 1941 formally instructed ships approaching the Bay to stop and make contact with the outer guard ship for identification. Only after permission had been given would they be allowed to proceed. The only ships exempted were those already registered by local pilots. This relieved some of the burden from the outer guard ship, which was pressed with a growing number of vessels ordered to seek safe anchorage in Hampton Roads at night to avoid prowling U-boats.[79]

In addition to the outer guard ship, an inner guard was established in mid-December 1941 along the channel inside the Capes which consisted of only two 75-foot patrol craft. These two ships plus the outer guard ship were the only patrols available in the defensive sea area until April 1942 when additional vessels were obtained to augment them.[80]

Another addition to these defenses came with the arrival of an examination ship in January 1942. The USCG *Jackson*, the first to take on this assignment, was ordered to stop and board any suspicious vessels including those from foreign and neutral ports. This action was expected to deter anyone from aiding U-boats whether by design or accident. The *Jackson* was soon replaced by the lightship USCG *Diamond Shoals* (LV-105), which was anchored north of the entrance channel (36_56'56N", 76_01'15W"). The *Diamond Shoals* served well in this capacity until 20 July 1944, when a passing tugboat and its tow rammed and sank her. Having an examination vessel on station was so crucial that she was replaced the next day by another lightship, the LV-81.[81]

Even before the war, the Navy knew that the appearance of enemy mines in the Fifth Naval District, such as those eventually laid by the *U-701*, was a real possibility. During World War I, German mines were placed at Thimble Shoals, near the entrance of the Chesapeake Bay, in the area around Buoy 2CB at Cape Henry, and in the area just south of Winter Quarter Shoal. Consequently, these areas were included in the planned mine sweeps during World War II, in addition to sweeps of Parramore Bank, Lookout Shoal, Diamond Shoal, Lookout Bight, and the Chesapeake Capes.

Considering the immense size of the area to be patrolled, such as the 12-mile gap between the Capes, the task of keeping the sea lanes free of enemy mines, plus the occasional "friendly" mine which "walked" from its field, was almost an impossible job. Throughout the war, the Fifth Naval District rarely seemed to have enough minesweepers to patrol all these areas adequately. However, through good organization and tight scheduling, inspections were carried out frequently enough to ensure a marginal degree of safety for the merchant fleet.[82]

One means of maximizing minesweeping was the establishment of swept channels. Rear Admiral J. K. Taussig, second Commandant of the Fifth Naval District, was certain the enemy would mine these waters once war began. Specifications for the establishment of swept channels off the Virginia Capes were made known on 25 June 1941; however, it wasn't until 18 December 1943 that the commandant had his five minesweepers in business with a properly charted channel.

Earlier attempts by the Navy at marking such a channel with permanent buoys never succeeded as the channel was changed frequently in response to the level of traffic, U-boat contacts, and sinkings that created a hazard to maritime traffic. The changing channels were too often a harrowing challenge to local pilots, and on more than one occasion created confusion among coastwise merchant ships. By 24 July 1943, Commandant Leahy of the Fifth Naval District simplified the entire system by creating a single swept channel for both incoming and outgoing ships. This channel was kept as straight as possible, which eliminated the need for complex changes. Just as important, the maintenance of only one swept channel enabled the minesweepers to truly maximize their efforts.[83]

Captain Linwood Hudgins, a Mathews County, Virginia, native and veteran Coast Guard buoy tender officer, recalled "laying out the course" for the swept channel.

"During the war, Fort Story could activate the mines. And coming in from sea, you had to come in through the minefield which was buoyed off and controlled by the Harbor Entrance Command at Fort Story. And I put the buoys down in that mineswept channel. Every time we went past Cape Henry, we would use the swept channel."[84] Holding a contemporary chart of Hampton Roads and Chesapeake Bay, Hudgins described the channel's direction by tracing it with his forefinger.

"085 from C-B Buoy off to the 50-mile curve." As he shifted charts, he explained that the original Navy-planned channels were simply too complicated. "The one I laid out was a straight line," he explained. "There were still some mines laying on the bottom around that channel and some wrecks too," he added.

"When they (USN) began an attempt at what they called a swept channel, they put too many turns in it. So then they asked the Coast Guard to do it and emphasized that they wanted a course so they could bring the ships directly into the harbor. The Coast Guard gave me the job which was in 1942. It was just before we got our radar, gyro compass and that kind of equipment. Once the war started, however, they started pouring it on. But when I drew my line, I did it on a piece of paper and did my calculations by hand without a computer, depending instead on my logarithms and tables.

"First thing starting out all we had was a magnetic compass. So you know what I did? The first buoy I put down, you get angles from the shore. The buoys are five miles apart the minute I got out of sight of land. The next thing I did after that was go over to Norfolk and ask the Coast Geodetic folks how to run a line off shore when you can't see land. "How do you get a position out there if you can't see land? I had an old-fashioned sextant from which to take a reading from the sun, but I couldn't get a fix in feet from that. We didn't have a LORAN system like they have today. So they gave me a form and told me that it takes two people to do this now. You bring in the angles of the sun, use decline and incline angle at the same time and work it out by logarithms. And figure it on paper by using sines and cosines and all that stuff. I didn't have any computers or calculators as I said before to do the work for me. All I had were the Bowditch tables to help me.

"I remember a PT-Boat coming into the first 'so-called' swept. Then he reported to the Navy that he couldn't navigate the channel.

"My commanding officer called me into Coast Guard headquarters and said, 'Go back out there and straighten out that channel.' And I go back out there and go over all my lines and come back in. And I said, 'Captain, that's the best I can do.' Then two days later, the battleship USS *Mississippi* came in that same channel and they wrote a letter of commendation to the Coast Guard saying, 'That's the best one on the East Coast!'"

Captain Hudgins never received any written recognition for his achievement, but he was called into the Coast Guard commandant's office in Norfolk and given personal praise for his effort. "Now the Navy could protect the ships against German magnetic mines," said Hudgins. "That was the whole idea, to give the ships coming in and going out of the port a guaranteed route. Then I returned to my job of keeping the buoys lit that marked the swept channel. They could last a year as far as fuel was concerned, but you never knew when someone might run into them or they could just go out."

Hudgins could not remember any sabotage attempt on the swept channel or for that matter any other channel buoys or markers his ship served except for the ludicrous attempt by Navy aviators to occasionally use one of them for target practice. One particular incident Hudgins recalled with some detail off the Outer Banks of North Carolina.

"They would practice by using them as targets to bomb and machine gun. 'Psssst, pssst, psst, pst.'" Hudgins, imitating the sound of a machine gun firing, pointed out on a chart the exact location of the incident. "I had a 'Nun' buoy on it which is painted red, shaped like a Nun's habit, always on the right side of the channel.

"Well we go down there and one's missing. We began to drag for it with a great big grappling. Finally I caught it! Bullet holes all through it. Then those planes would come over you and dive. They didn't shoot at us, but you knew from that point that it was our planes that had done the damage.

"One of them (strafed most likely by an A-28 operating from a nearby station in North Carolina) was sunk down here off Oregon Inlet," Hudgins said as he drew his finger along the flight path of the airplane. "I stayed down there a whole week trying to mark the location," he added.

Captain Hudgins also remembered the frustration of marking the resting places of U-boat victims in the graveyard of the Atlantic. "We didn't have at that point any way to stop them. You can't stop a U-boat with a buoy boat! To my knowledge, in the beginning, we had one old World War I, four-stack destroyer deployed along this coast. We simply didn't have the ships to fight them. We just didn't have them, that's all! Remember—we had two wars to start with!

"Even though, looking back, we could have blacked out our ships earlier. And all we had to do was turn out the lights on shore! I don't see why they couldn't have done that on shore. They dimmed the lighthouses down, they dimmed the radio beacon lights down too.

"And then we tried to mobilize all the small boats we could find Old fishing boats, Chesapeake Bay steamers, menhaden boats—they would outfit guns on them as well.

"However I still saw evidence of the slaughter that was still going on everyday. I marked the charts, as I said earlier, where they were all sunk—all the way down our coast, and then I had to continue on another chart because there were so many.

"But our swept channel worked as it was swept every day. And we also had patrol boats working. But one (Degen's *U-701*) came in awfully close before the swept channel was put in.

"In those days the Coast Guard had 125-foot cutters. They had quite a few of them—about two or three in this district. One of them had a Chief Warrant officer as the skipper. And this submarine [*U-701*] came up off Cape Henry. And the Coast Guard skipper fainted, fell out. And the executive officer had to take charge. And while all this was going on, the submarine submerged, and there wasn't a shot fired! The skipper of course was taken off and put ashore."

Changeable weather conditions in the Fifth Naval District often presented more real dangers to smaller ships like Hudgin's *Orchid* than did enemy submarines, as they were assigned rescue duties in addition to the upkeep of channel buoys. One particular incident stands out in his memory.

"I was anchored in Lynnhaven Road. One night we hit a southwester. I had two of the largest buoys we had—38-foot buoys—on deck. The storm was so bad I couldn't do anything once I got out but drop anchor and wait for the wind to drop out so I could go to a fish trawler that had signaled that she was in distress off Currituck Lighthouse—then came that order, 'Proceed and assist.' But I had these two big buoys strapped on and it was too rough to go to sea so I figured I'd go to Little Creek and unload the buoys.

"My executive officer said, 'Are you going to go out past Cape Henry tonight during the storm?' I said yes. So we went on past Cape Henry out into rough water. And went on down the beach. And when we got on down the beach, my chief warrant officer saw this flash bulb flashing 'SOS.' So I told him to turn on the searchlight and shine it in the direction of the SOS signal. And he said, 'Oh no captain—you can't run on the searchlight—that might be a submarine!'

"I said well we're supposed to be looking for a fishing trawler and that's where he's supposed to be. My executive officer still wouldn't go along, so I turned on the searchlight myself and there he was. A fisherman was standing there flashing 'SOS, SOS' with a flashlight. His net was all caught up in his propeller. So we got a line on him and towed him back to Cape Henry.

"But what started this story was that same night a Coast Guard patrol boat was on station in the swept channel. And he came in to Cape Henry, decided it was too rough out there. He came on in to Norfolk the next day—too rough for even the enemy that night!

"It wasn't anything to be called out at 0200 or 0300 in the morning about some buoy light that was out. Didn't make any difference—snow or rain. I remember getting a phone call, 'All the numbered buoys are extinguished, proceed and relight'—with a snow storm—these are the facts. I couldn't see the buoys until daylight, but we'd start off in the middle of a storm anyway! Sometimes it was too rough to lower a boat or get a man over the buoy. But if you didn't go, you were on the carpet when you reported in."

"You had to give your recognition signals to Cape Henry to get in no matter what. You had to use your blinker lights. By the way, the recognition signals would change every two hours. That was another thing—they were secret—kept in the safe on the boat—had to go in to Norfolk to get them."

In addition to working the swept channel into Hampton Roads, the *Orchid* was also sent down to Cape Fear in 1942 to lay out a second swept channel. Even though the *Orchid* never participated in an actual U-boat contact or attack, Captain Hudgins carried with pride the memory of "his" swept channel until his death in 1993.[85]

Another effort undertaken by the Navy to prevent U-boats from entering the harbors was the addition of antisubmarine nets and booms. Once again their necessity was evident even before war was declared. Commandant Simons advised Admiral Harold R. Stark, the Chief of Naval Operations, a month before the attack on Pearl Harbor, that the Navy should begin placing antisubmarine nets in the Chesapeake Bay entrance. Nonetheless, it was not until after war began that the nets were finally fixed in place. The distance and strong current at the Bay's entrance between Cape Henry and Cape Charles forced their installation farther east, right at the entrance of Hampton Roads between Willoughby Spit and Old Point Comfort. Installation of the Hampton Roads net began the day after Pearl Harbor. By the middle of December, the fixed obstructions and netting were complete. A net gate was installed and operated by a Navy tugboat. In addition, an antimotorboat boom with an operational gate was in place by 23 January 1942. Another antisubmarine net with four-foot mesh was later fitted under the boom across the harbor entrance. Completed by 21 September 1942, this net was particularly designed to discourage German midget submarines.

At the same time, antitorpedo nets were placed at specific locations deemed vulnerable by the Navy; around the piers at the Naval Operating Base, and in front of the drydocks at the Norfolk Naval Shipyard and the Newport News Shipbuilding and Drydock Company. Additional modifications offered protection from aerial torpedo attack. The anti-torpedo nets were maintained until November 1943, when it was considered safe to remove them. They were kept in storage, however, "in a state of readiness in case of future emergency."[86]

Antisubmarine nets were also installed at the entrance to the York River. During World War I, the York River was used as a fleet anchorage. Although it was never similarly used during World War II, the Navy protected it. Installation began on 26 December 1941, with the antisubmarine nets, antimotorboat booms, and other fixed obstructions completed by early

March 1942. They were eventually removed by 17 September 1943, when the presumed threat to the region had dramatically decreased.[87]

To function properly, the Hampton Roads U-boat defense network needed coordination under one administrative head. In a response to instructions from the War Department on 19 December 1941, a Joint Operations Center (JOC) was created and located in the Naval Operating Base, Norfolk. In this single center, one supervisory command could orchestrate all the activity in the region.[88] By 20 June 1942, the JOC was operational, providing office space for the administration of all inshore patrols, convoys, and routing. In addition, the Army had watch officers in the same room with the Navy controllers. Adjacent to this room was Operational Intelligence and Communications. With the direct participation of the Army watch officers, a close working relationship evolved between the Navy and Army as planned before the war.[89]

Once convoys were finally established, they proved, as Admiral Doenitz predicted, one of the best defenses against U-boats. The Navy learned from its harsh experiences with the transatlantic convoys that U-boats would rather avoid them, preferring easier targets such as a lone cargo ship, which presented little risk of detection and retaliation. Even before the war, the Navy knew that an escorted convoy system was needed for East Coast operations, but again, due to the country's heavy commitments in the Pacific and an already overburdened use of escorts for transatlantic convoys, few ships were available for coastal convoys.[90]

Soon after hostilities began, however, Admiral King ordered Rear Admiral Andrews on 12 February 1942 to prepare a plan to protect shipping along the Eastern Sea Frontier. After evaluating the situation, Andrews reported to King and recommended against using coastal convoys at that time due to the lack of escort vessels. He argued correctly that a convoy without sufficient protection actually made a bigger and better target for the U-boats. On 6 March 1942, King officially agreed with Andrews's analysis, but urged the implementation of convoys as soon as possible.[91]

In the interim, Andrews implemented a temporary solution that called for the use of district convoys, or "Bucket Brigades." This required moving ships from anchorage to anchorage with whatever escorts were available in each district; in other words, handing off a convoy at the district border to another escort and then so on down the line. Gathering ships into bucket brigades also gave intelligence officers an opportunity to maximize their dispersal of information on the current movements of German U-boats and in turn, interview a number of merchant skippers at once on possible sightings of submarines before they arrived.

Former U.S. Coast Guard officer Swink added his evaluation of the early application of the Bucket Brigade.

"Sometime in April 1942, we formed what became known as the 'Bucket Brigade,' which was comprised of merchant ships from Hampton Roads that were grouped into a small convoy. Their escort group, maybe just two ships, would take them out a little before daybreak to get down to Lookout Bight by dark. We had a submarine net located there to protect them which allowed us to patrol outside till the next morning. The next morning we would take them further south where at a designated spot, we handed them off to another escort group. Normally we would pick up a new group heading north to Hampton Roads. Then we would repeat the mission by taking the inbound group to Lookout Bight and wait until morning to bring them into Norfolk. The 'Bucket Brigade' was quite successful and soon was used along the entire coast. It gave the convoys the added advantage of running only during daylight hours and then going in somewhere for protection at night."[92]

Part of the success Swink described can be attributed to the dedication and hard work of members of the Virginia Pilots Association, who, as mentioned before, also sailed as commissioned officers under the command of the United States Coast Guard. Thus the pilot boat *Virginia* also became an official part of the growing fleet of ASW-assigned boats and ships in the Fifth Naval District. During the entire war, and certainly because of the advantage of the convoy system, the pilots were officially credited with boarding approximately 1,000 ships per month.[93]

At the height of the war, pilot records indicate that a convoy arrived at the Virginia Capes every ten days. According to pilot archives, the commodore in charge would order the inbound ships to form into two lines. The north side ships would split off and head for Baltimore with a Maryland pilot, while the remaining ships sailed into Hampton Roads with a Virginia pilot.[94]

This scene was repeated when another outbound convoy was assembled in Hampton Roads. Even though junior pilots helped alleviate some of the concentration, senior pilots were called on often to make several trips to Cape Henry, after which they returned by launch to Norfolk where another outbound convoy awaited them. The convoy was then divided into a left and a right column. They had a span of six minutes between the ship immediately ahead, and three minutes from the next ship in the other column.[95]

When the convoy finally arrived at Cape Henry, the pilots were put ashore by surfboats, driven to Norfolk, and sent aboard yet another convoy. Also employed in this effort to get the pilots rapidly from Cape Henry to the Norfolk Naval Base were two confiscated rum runners, which, in decent weather, would cover the 18-mile trip in 35 minutes carrying up to 12 pilots. Once at the base, they were met by smaller launches that dispersed the pilots to the appropriate ships.[96]

One record kept by pilot Captain Roy B. Dawson, Jr., shows that from 27 June 1943 to 29 March 1945, 28 convoys were formed and sent outbound from Hampton Roads. Captain Dawson's account also shows a neat and orderly transition of ships, with columns in the records showing the number in sortie, section (right or left), ship's name, convoy signal number, estimated time to pass Cape Henry, international call, and the pilot's name who sailed a particular ship. Still it must have been extremely challenging when the number of ships in those 28 convoys totaled 1,494![97]

For their contributions during the war both as convoy escorts and surveillance agents, the Virginia pilots were recognized in 1946 by a citation presented to them by the Commandant of the Fifth Naval District, Admiral W.L. Ainsworth, who wrote, "…for outstanding service as pilots during the period of World War II. The members of the Virginia Pilots Association displayed exceptional skill and organizing ability in maintaining a safe and expeditious movement of shipping in the Hampton Roads area…on an accelerated schedule of both convoyed and independent sailings."[98]

Beginning on 27 March 1943, cargo ships traveled primarily during the day, and pulled into a safe anchorage at night, the time when most U-boats were on the prowl. Safe anchorages were usually located around natural coastal features such as the Virginia Capes. The Fifth Naval District strengthened these by placing a netted anchorage west of Cape Lookout, North Carolina, and erecting a mined anchorage southwest of Cape Hatteras, North Carolina. Such anchorages were an excellent retreat for those crippled ships that were forced to drop out of a convoy.[99]

Captain Linwood Hudgins recalled that the minefields were located in conjunction with the safe anchorages of the convoys. "We then located minefields off Cape Hatteras and Ocracoke," said Hudgins. "They were laid after the first one in Hampton Roads to serve the convoys coming up and down the coast. The convoys would come in here for safety at night, anchor, and then come on up the coast in the daylight. The anchorages had buoys and a lightship with an opening through the minefield. I was sent there to check those buoys all the time."[100]

By May 1942, substantial progress had been made towards implementing a real convoy system. First, the transatlantic convoys were restructured to maximize economy in the use of escorts, thereby releasing a number of American destroyers for other duties. The Navy also received help from the British, who contributed four antisubmarine trawlers, plus ten heavily armed corvettes. With the addition of new American-built antisubmarine ships, Andrews began coastal convoys on 13 May 1942. By then the ascendancy ASW battle for the Fifth Naval District had begun to shift noticeably toward the U.S. Navy. On 14 May, Virginia was for the first time linked with a regular coastal convoy to Key West, Florida. The convoys were extended farther along the East Coast and were continually reinforced with more ships and aircraft. The so-called "Bucket Brigade" paid immediate dividends with a noticeable decline in the number of ships sunk. Records reveal that in April, before the convoys began, 23 ships were sunk in the Eastern Sea Frontier; however, in May, once the convoy system was in effect, only 5 were sunk. The number increased again to 13 in June, but fell dramatically to 3 in July. By the end of 1942, each U-boat's success rate had been cut in half.[101] The convoys continued until 28 May 1945 when a joint announcement was made by the U.S. Navy and the British Admiralty. "Effective at 2001 this date, Eastern Standard Time (0001 May 29 Greenwich Mean Time), no further trade convoys will be sailed. Merchant ships by night will burn navigation lights at full brilliancy and need not darken ship."[102]

In addition to the convoys, the Navy required commercial fishermen to keep a lookout for enemy submarines and aircraft. Fishing boats were formally recognized as part of the ASW network in a memorandum by Rear Admiral Andrews on 7 April 1942. In Andrews's plan, the Navy was called on to find reliable crews who could be trusted with confidential information. The fishermen were also given radio telephones for rapid communication. Seventeen skippers and crews were found by the middle of June 1942. Their trawlers were promptly enlisted, given radios, and put into service.[103]

Soon after the fishing boats joined in, virtually every offshore boat became involved in the program. In the Fifth Naval District, an astounding 143 vessels were equipped by the Navy with radio telephones. Fishing vessels that seasonally entered the Fifth Naval District were similarly equipped and joined the local ASW effort.

The entire program clearly proved its worth on 13 April 1942 when Captain Quinn of the Hampton, Virginia, trawler *Sea Romer* sighted an enemy U-boat. He plotted the U-boat's location as being about 20 miles east of Currituck. After he radioed the coordinates to the Naval Operating Base in Norfolk, Virginia, attack aircraft were on the scene less than an hour later. Even though the U-boat had fled the area by this time, it is entirely probable that it monitored the *Sea Romer's* transmission and realized that trouble was on its way. Regardless of the outcome, the incident did prove that fishing vessels could be an extra set of eyes for the Navy.[104]

Another idea, which would have supplemented patrols in the Fifth Naval District, called for the use of "Coastal Pickets." Rear Admiral Andrews became an early proponent of the concept, which called for a diverse collection of once privately owned yachts considered rugged enough for both defensive and offensive patrol duty put to sea. Although an earlier attempt at using small yachts as "Anti-Submarine Lookouts" in the Fifth Naval District demonstrated that none of the craft obtained could withstand the extreme conditions of the Atlantic, Commandant Simons ordered the district Coast Guard Office to assemble as many private yachts as possible for service in the Coast Guard Temporary Reserve. On 27 June 1942, 16 small yachts set out on a shakedown cruise, with 2 ships assigned to eight stations just outside the Virginia Capes for a 24-hour patrol. However, high seas outside the bay prevented any of the ships from completing their patrols. Some never reached their station, and wisely headed back before they got into more serious trouble. Others tried vainly to stay at their stations, but were eventually forced to return. These boats simply were not suitable for the task. However some of the boats were kept for duty in the calmer waters of the Chesapeake Bay and found a role in the Local Defense Force as part of the inner guard.[105]

Regardless of this dismal showing in the Fifth Naval District, Rear Admiral Andrews on 14 July 1942 ordered the local commandants to begin organizing and deploying yachts and other private boats for coastal picket duty. As most of the power boats in the Fifth Naval District had already been put into service by the Navy or Coast Guard, only sailing yachts were available. Twenty-three out of a proposed 54 were acquired along with their crews as part of the Coast Guard Reserve. Intended to be more than just observers, they were equipped with removable 30-caliber machine guns and portable underwater listening gear. Even depth charges were considered, but only one schooner was swift enough to deploy a depth charge set for 100 feet and get away safely. Consequently, it was the only one so armed. Unfortunately, the name of this schooner is not listed in the Navy records for this event.

The first patrols of the coastal pickets, which began 7 September 1942, operated out of Little Creek Section Base, and took up station 30 miles east of Winter Quarter Shoals. Depending on the weather, the sailing yachts actually made it to their stations and performed patrol duty. However, no contact with a U-boat was made. On 1 December 1942, Rear Admiral Andrews issued a General Patrol Doctrine for all the "Coastal Pickets" that was written as if the yachts were professional naval submarine destroyers.

Under this doctrine, if one of these armed sailboats came into contact with a U-boat, it was expected not just to report its location, but to attack in the following vigorous manner:  When an enemy submarine is sighted on the surface, close to within your gun range and open machine gun fire to clear personnel from his bridge.  Prevent his crew from manning their guns. Keep your guns ready for immediate surface attack at all times.  Do not attract his attention by firing at too long a range.  The element of surprise is a major factor in successful action.[106]

Joseph Kelly, a Norfolk attorney, recalled his days aboard the coastal pickets in the Fifth Naval District. "We were under the general command of Admiral Andrews of course, but whether he had the slightest interest in us, I do not know.  I myself did not know whether we would be of any value.  But then I had several months of training when I did consider that we might indeed be very discouraging to the German offensive and U-boats safely appearing on the surface without being spotted."[107]

At any rate, Kelly found that he would be accepted by the coastal pickets even with his poor eyesight.  Admitting that he literally knew nothing about the military, he took the rate of specialist under his first skipper, Rucker Ryland, who came in as a Chief Boatswain's Mate (First Class) and, like Kelly, had been previously turned down by other services because of an injury.  However, both men had considerable experience in yachting, and had sailed together earlier as members of the former Urbanna Yacht Club, now the Fishing Bay Yacht Club on the Chesapeake Bay.  In fact both sailed the yacht *Nighthawk* which later became the coastal picket CGR-2008.

After resigning from the state Attorney General's office and enlisting in the coastal pickets, Kelly began his naval career on the 83-foot CGR-2008.  He subsequently joined Ryland on the CGR-2022, a Block Island racing boat that, according to Kelly, had belonged to a descendant of the great American navigator Nathaniel Bowditch.  It was on this vessel that he sailed his first series of "five days out and two days in port" patrol rotations from Little Creek, Virginia, along with six others.  According to Kelly, the coastal pickets were painted "battleship gray" and identified by a large designation on the sail, similar to pilot boats, which read "CGR" and the number.  "On the top of the mast," said Kelly, "there was a light in a cup in the truck (rigging) at the top of the mast so that only aircraft could see you and no surface boat could see you.  Of course we were blacked out and there was always danger of running into another ship."[108]

The Navy depended on the experienced seamanship of these sailors and yachtsmen like Kelly, as there was no training before deployment.  They simply reported to a boat and the skipper had a set of orders to go out to a certain area. Navy intelligence briefings were also overlooked, which left experienced seaman like Kelly incredulous. "No, we didn't have any idea from intelligence what we were looking for, but come to think of it, you know on an 83-foot cutter—her bridge looks a hell of a lot like a conning tower to me!...But we weren't told a damn thing about the U-boats."[109]

"Weather restricted us naturally," said Kelly. "We operated out of Little Creek at first, during that first winter of the war, and then out of Ocracoke (on the Outer Banks of North Carolina) with the 2028. Then, with three other boats who had started with us, we sailed from Little Creek again.

"There was a base already at Little Creek to supply our boats. The Ocracoke [Ocracoke Island, North Carolina] base on the other hand had nothing there except for a few fishermen. We lived on our boat until they built a supply and repair facility. There was no difference at that time between being in the Navy and the Coast Guard. However, we always identified ourselves as United States Coast Guard Reserves."[110]

Kelly recalled that during the first weeks, they passed their time fitting out their boat, painting, getting the rigging out, adding ratlines, and over-hauling their auxiliary engines. At the same time, Naval officers from the Norfolk Operating Base came down to the private yard during the overhaul period and went over basic navigation with them. Of the two yachts being fitted out for patrol, Kelly remembered that only one had a sextant and that his had a binnacle compass on board. Recalling that he met picket patrol seamen who sailed from New Jersey and off New England later in the war, he criticized the lack of training he first received and called his first boat "ill-equipped as any of the others."

At any rate, this was a desperate time, and getting any armed ship to sea against the Germans offered some relief, even though the weapons complement was sometimes inadequate. "There was just one schooner in our area that was large enough for depth charge racks," said Kelly. "The problem was that the schooner couldn't get away fast enough from the depth charges and would have blown herself up as well."[111]

"That same schooner was armed with the hedgehog—a pure rocket that came from the ASW unit in New York. The hedgehog was the preferred method to fight submarines, and gave us a vastly better batting average against the U-boats."[112]

However, as Kelly emphasized, most picket boats were only lightly armed. "Our first deployment was delayed and we were sent (from Little Creek) back to the Coast Guard base called the buoy yard in Portsmouth, Virginia, and then in South Norfolk and given the machine guns on board. One was a 30-caliber machine gun for fighting U-boats, but they could have been used on (German) saboteurs like those put ashore on the coast of New Jersey.[113]

"Some of the machine guns were of World War I vintage—Marlin machine guns that had been attached to the wings of the old biplanes. They were the most awful things to keep in firing order. You had to have one man who worked solely on those damned things. On 2022, we had machine gun mounts just aft of the standing rigging and a British-made Lewis gun with a big round drum for ammunition. The British machine gun was far more reliable. We also had service rifles and side arms as well. We also had a 'Tommy Gun' or submachine gun."[114]   One has to remember that the real value of the coastal pickets was not to engage a submarine, despite orders to the contrary, but rather to spot the enemy and get the word back as fast as possible to headquarters, from which adequate forces could be called in. Kelly emphasized that the coastal pickets were not only on the lookout for German raiders, but were also keenly aware of the dangers presented by other American ASW efforts and the inherent dangers of going out to sea in the first place.

"There was the minefield channel off Cape Henry," recalled Kelly, "and there was also the Army minefield, which was keyboard controlled, at the Harbor Entrance Control Post at Fort Story, Cape Henry, as well as the Navy minefield which was on the other side near Cape Charles.[115]

"We also worried about hitting one of our own contact mines. In fact, one night while we were coming home, I think I did. We were coming in quick from an approaching hurricane and got called in and went sailing both sails to Chincoteague with a very light breeze from the north. Got a little careless about keeping on a straight line for the minefield channel (swept channel). I know I hit one as I could hear it scrape along the side. That sound was unmistakable."[116]

Kelly remembered that he wasn't using the auxiliary engine during the incident, but was depending on his sails as they were running faster under canvas and were low on fuel following an overnight patrol. "And I was in a hurry," he admitted.[117]

"I hit that thing and it sounded like we were running over an oil barrel. I know I scraped that mine from one end of my boat to the other. We were making a good speed with all our canvas on a broad reach, but you just can't maneuver a sailboat like you can a motorboat. Hitting that mine is one tale of the war I will never forget!"[118]

As Kelly recalled, other coastal patrols were not so lucky, especially when it came to fighting the oldest shipboard enemy—fire. "You know, we did lose one coastal boat that just caught fire and burned to the waterline and it was awful close to 2022. It was in the summer of 1943. The galley was coated with grease—the gas range was using propane—it just exploded with a ball of flame. There was another ship that had a galley fire too, but there was a very fine young fellow named Joe Nunally, a machinist mate, and he was quick as a cat with a 20-pound $CO_2$ extinguisher and didn't have to take two steps to get to it. Then one big blast snuffed out the fire. But the other ship was burned to the waterline. It happened just at Winter Quarter Shoal, almost in Maryland waters."[119]

Despite these mishaps, the coastal pickets were adequately equipped, as Kelly remembered, to detect German U-boats. "We had a hydrophone which we would trail overboard 50 or 60 feet. It was shaped like a big bologna. It was attached to a very heavy-duty extension cord and you would trail it behind the boat. We could hear the bottom noises very distinctly. We did have a contact which I reported. The only contact I ever made.[120]

"We had a boy in the crew who had been to sound school in the Navy. And he was striking for sonarman. I don't really know how he wound up in our crew, but he did. At any rate when we made contact, he said, 'I know that is a sub!' And he was positive. But there was nothing in sight in that dark night. However, we immediately radioed our position from our 50-watt transmitter—our call signal being 'By George Zero One.' Then someone else had some doubts about it so they rolled a few depth charges. Never had so many bumps in my life! I am sure there was nothing there."[121]

When they weren't out on patrol, the CGR 2022 was moored at Little Creek or at the coast patrol's other section base farther up the Chesapeake Bay at Solomon's Island. According to Kelly, the word 'base' meant a headquarters building, officers' houses, and a machine shop. Since there were no barracks, the six-man crew slept in makeshift berthing stripped from staterooms.

Once they prepared to get underway, two watchstanders took their positions forward and aft, since they were not equipped with either radar or sonar at the time. Kelly stated that reporting for orders was done by telephone from Little Creek to the Harbor Entrance Control Post. "You asked for the duty officer and the skipper made the report to him," said Kelly. "There was nothing in writing. At the end of every patrol, the skipper's first job when he stepped ashore was to call the Harbor Entrance Command and give the official report.[122]

"Our orders came from the Commanding Officer at section base headquarters or the Coast Guard assignment officer at Little Creek. He also furnished us with supplies and the like. Once we were at Ocracoke, they would be sent down to the pier by bicycle messenger. And he was always referred to as 'Vinegar Charlie.' The signal to return to base was 'Sugar Charlie.' But 'Vinegar Charlie' always meant it was time to sail."[123]

In addition to radio, some of the coastal pickets carried a more exotic form of signal equipment that heralded back to the days of World War I. "During the second summer of the war—1943—in the 2022," Kelly recalled, "from Little Creek, we were taking carrier pigeons to release by daylight since they could not navigate at night. They returned to their cages at Fort Story where their owner, the Army Signal Corps, would collect the messages. We would release them just before starting in. It was fun to watch them as they tracked on a radio signal of some kind, what we knew as the proper course from 20 miles off shore!"[124]

Apart from the interlude with the carrier pigeons, Kelly described sailing in the coastal pickets as a solitary affair. "I don't know how often they had boats out there. The first several months of the war we would sail alone and never see another coast picket vessel or another American ship of any kind. After the first several months, we would sail in pairs. I remember towards the end of the war, my friend Captain Ryland and I separated and he took command of an old 75-foot Coast Guard cutter. Then we would sail out together. Once we got pushed by a storm almost to Cape May. It was a southwester and it forced the larger Coast Guard cutter off station and back to Little Creek . . .We did sail off the Eastern shore on occasion to where the big convoys were being built. Once there was a collision with one of our boats that left one of our coastal picket sailors drowned."[125]

However, these incidents were rare, and, despite their age and condition, a good number of the coastal pickets, armaments and other ASW equipment removed, were returned to civilian service after the war; Kelly's CGR-2008 survived and was returned to familiar waters at the Urbanna Yacht Club on Chesapeake Bay.

It is fortunate that U-boat activity had declined in the areas where the coastal pickets were on patrol, and that none of these sailing yachts ever had to engage a U-boat. The weather, more than the enemy, proved more than most could handle. Several times one of the sailboats was reported missing for days until it was finally able to ride out the storm and radio in. Some carried carrier pigeons as Kelly mentioned earlier, which in one case enabled a missing boat to relay its location after it became lost in a storm!

However, most of the aging yachts that were finally commissioned as coastal pickets spent almost as much time in repair as they did underway. Kelly remembered that on the CGR-2008, "We had the block crack open in the auxiliary engine. So we had to bring her back to Dunn's Marine at

West Norfolk (near Craney Island, Portsmouth, Virginia) the first day of patrol. She had an old six-cylinder, gasoline engine...plenty of problems. Of course some were better than others. The 83-footers had the big Sterling gas engines and others had the Pratt and Whitneys which were more reliable."[126]

Never viable weapons of war, these sailing relics recaptured but for a moment some of the sailing gracefulness of earlier men-of-war. "On a broad reach in ideal conditions," Kelly said, "I would time our boat as we passed the buoys on the mine-swept channel—and by rule of thumb estimated we were making 10 knots!"[127] Not even the grace and speed of these once-famous yachts could answer the needs of modern ASW.

The plan envisioned by Rear Admiral Andrews never really worked. With only sailing yachts available and few volunteers to man them, there was no way it could be successfully accomplished. Nonetheless, it is quite possible that they did harass some U-boats. On several occasions the coastal pickets equipped with sonar picked up a target, but before they could reach the area, it was gone. The U-boats, upon hearing the sonar's "ping," had ample time to withdraw. The Coastal Picket program was dropped on 9 November 1943.[128]

Another effort by the Navy which met with equally poor results was the implementation of "Q-ships." These were heavily armed and armored freighters, camouflaged to look harmless enough to lure an unsuspecting U-boat in close on the surface. Once the enemy was within range, the Q-ship crew would pull away the covers that hid their guns and open fire. The idea of using Q-ships was not new, as they had already been used in World War I. At the beginning of World War II when there was an obvious shortage of warships on the East Coast, the idea of using Q-ships was reintroduced.

President Roosevelt approved their deployment, which was endorsed by Admiral King on 20 January 1942. Shortly thereafter, Rear Admiral Andrews received orders to carry out "Project LQ," and the search for suitable ships began. Finally three were purchased by the Navy. They consisted of two 3,200-ton freighters, the SS *Carolyn*, and *Evelyn*, and a trawler named the *Wave*. Under a cloak of secrecy, the three ships were renamed; the *Wave* became the *Eagle*, the *Evelyn* the *Asterion*, and the *Carolyn* the *Atik*. Under the tightest security possible, the Portsmouth Navy Yard, New Hampshire, converted them into Q-ships. *Asterion* and *Atik* received four 4-inch guns, four 50-caliber machine guns, six depth charge throwers, and sonar. The *Eagle* was similarly equipped, except it received only one 4-inch gun.[129] The end product was an innocent-looking trawler and two seemingly unarmed freighters. It was hoped that an approaching U-boat would not bother to submerge when approaching such easy prey. On 23 March 1942, all three Q-ships left New Hampshire for a shakedown cruise. The cargo holds of the freighters were converted into life-sustaining floats by being filled with cork. The crews on the ships were all Navy volunteers who knew that their mission was "Top Secret." This meant that if they did run into a U-boat, they would probably find themselves on their own without assistance. As far as the Naval Districts knew, they were just typical merchant vessels. If they got into real trouble, help was not guaranteed.

Four days after their departure, the *Atik* was 300 miles east of the Chesapeake Bay when it encountered the *U-123* under the command of Reinhard Hardegan. The *Atik* was the first and last of the group to engage an enemy U-boat. What followed served to mark the beginning of the end of "Project LQ." The final two radio messages from the *Atik* were received 26 March 1942, beginning at 2055 Eastern War Time, or 1255 Greenwich Civil Time. The first message was, "Latitude 3600 N. Longitude 7000 W. Burning forward not bad. Bearings from Monasquan 150 at 0053 Fire Island 146 at 0053." The second and last message was, "SOS SSS SOS SSS BT 00N 7000W. Approximately, SS *Carolyn* (*Atik's* original name) torpedo attack burning forward require assistance."[130] Admiral F.J. Horne wrote the following analysis of the incident:

> The most likely conjecture is that the *Atik* and a German submarine had an accidental night surface encounter in which the *Atik* was set afire by shell fire and the submarine submerged. Possibly the fire gave the submerged submarine a point of aim or she may have used sound, etc. In any event, the weather was on her side and she evidently got a quick torpedo hit on the *Atik*, perhaps in the engine room or magazine. It is quite possible that the submarine then surfaced and liquidated all survivors to assuage the curious sense of German justice. The debris found in the SOS area by plane and ship, bore certain identification marks peculiar to the *Atik*.[131]

On 9 April 1942, a German radio broadcast reported their sinking of a Q-ship off the coast. None of the 142-man crew survived.

The mysterious aura surrounding the Q-ship project created great consternation for the loved ones of the men lost aboard the *Atik*. The Navy's file on the incident contains several letters, telegrams, and memos concerning a search by a crewmember's parents, Mr. and Mrs. Paul H. Leonard. On

8 May 1942, the Leonards received a notice from the Navy that their son, Ensign Edwin Madison Leonard, was "missing following action in the performance of his duty and in the service of his country." On 29 June 1942, they learned that there was still no further information on their son. Finally, on 6 May 1944, they were notified that he was no longer classified as missing but was now presumed dead. On 15 June 1944, they were told that their son's Purple Heart and certificate were being forwarded.

The notices received by the Leonards did not tell how their son died. They were not to learn the details from the Navy until after the end of the war and then only after a steady barrage of letters. On 18 March 1946, the Navy Department in Washington, D.C., prepared a detailed response to their questions about the *Atik*. Only at this time was the secrecy surrounding the Q-ships finally lifted.

Despite all the stealth and preparation, the Q-ship project was a failure. Although the mission continued, no significant contacts were made, by any of the others, with the end result being that not a single U-boat was sunk.[132]

# CHAPTER 5

## *ATTACK TRAINERS*

Meanwhile the Navy's training effort was developing with local defenses manned by crews trained in acoustics at one of the Navy's two sound schools. The West Coast Sound School was located in San Diego, California. The East Coast Sound School was located at New London, Connecticut. Both were opened in 1939. In the autumn of 1940, the East Coast Sound School was moved to Key West, Florida, where the weather and sea conditions were better for sonar training.

In September 1940, after the Atlantic Squadron was re-organized into the Atlantic Fleet, control of the "sound" training program for the East Coast was placed under Commander Destroyers, Atlantic Fleet. Not only did the school train the officers and enlisted men, it also offered an opportunity to test thoroughly the World War I-vintage ships that had been recommissioned for use in the fleet. The school had four of the old flush-deck, four-stack destroyers. Equipped with sonar, the *Roper (DD147), Herbert Jacob Jones (DD130),* and *Dickerson (DD157)* made up the East Coast's ASW task force. One of these ships, the *Roper,* would have the experience of sinking the first U-boat off the East Coast during the war. The *Jacob Jones (DD61)* was not as lucky, having been sunk by the *U-578* on 28 February 1942.

The school also had three World War I-vintage submarines, or "R-boats." These aging ships could dive only as deep as the length of their hull with safety. Although they were of limited value to the Navy in combat, they made excellent practice targets for trainees. From 1 November 1939 to 30 September 1945, 10,594 enlisted men were trained as sonar operators, of which 8,970 were rated. From 1 November 1939 to 30 June 1945, 2,608 enlisted men were trained in materiel. From 1 January 1941 to 30 September 1945, the training program prepared 2,723 Sound Officers, 219 Materiel Officers, and 1,623 prospective commanding and executive officers.[133]

Instruction at Key West was intensive and not without danger. "The submarines were supposed to carry a total of 35 men including the students, but often they were forced to carry 50 or 60," said retired Navy Captain Harry Clark of Chesapeake, Virginia.[134] Clark, who served aboard one of the recommissioned submarines at the school, recalled that they were incredibly cramped and stuffy with only the air in the hull to breathe. "After submerging, the oxygen content dropped so much that if someone struck a match it would go out. No one smoked. In addition, the air usually reeked with diesel fumes and the acidic stench of the charging batteries. If the air became too foul, fresh air could be bled from a compressed tank while a compressor removed some of the polluted air."[135]

These trainees, however, did not have to live aboard the submarines for months at a time like the Germans. With approximately 44 men aboard, the stench aboard the German U-boats was far more intense. Forced to conserve water, the Germans were deprived of basic sanitary conditions. With only two "heads" or toilets aboard, one of which was filled with food when they set out, the men typically used buckets to relieve themselves, which were later emptied. Eating, sleeping, and working in this environment must have been miserable. Even on the surface, with all the hatches open, fresh air seldom penetrated to spaces below.

Captain Clark recalled that the old submarines had to be "coaxed along." On one occasion, 12 June, 1943, a trainer began its normal day with disastrous results. The *R-12 (SS89)* was cruising on the surface when, for unknown reasons, it plunged in a dive toward the bottom. Everyone aboard perished except for the men in the conning tower. Neither the survivors nor investigators were able to determine what caused the disaster.[136]

As the war progressed, ASW training was instituted in most naval districts, including the Fifth Naval District. All three of the Navy's section bases—Little Creek, Virginia; Morehead City, North Carolina; and Ocracoke, North Carolina—started training programs with the heaviest concentration of instruction centered at Little Creek. Curriculums covered such diverse areas as aircraft and ship recognition, night lookout training, minesweeping procedure, signaling, radio communications, gunnery, and radar. Simulation training was also furnished by an "attack teacher," an instructional device that mechanically presented problems one might encounter while attacking a U-boat.[137]

In addition to the on-going training, the Antisubmarine Warfare Unit of the Atlantic Fleet was created on 16 February 1942, with Captain Wilder D. Baker commanding officer. Originally headquartered in Boston, Massachusetts, Baker had the task of creating standards and guidelines to help administer ASW activities on the entire East Coast. Demanding critiques and close analyses of action and incident reports were a hallmark of the unit, with findings logged and forwarded to Washington for broad distribution. Within a month, Baker had his organization readied, and by early April the unit was moved to the headquarters of the Commander in Chief, U.S. Fleet.[138]

For the first time, manuals for sound operators and destroyer skippers were written, reviewed, printed, and distributed. Thoroughly tested standards were created for radar operators, which finally offered some continuity for equipment operation.[139]

This effort resulted in the creation of a standard ASW training doctrine that came to be called COMINCH Bulletin Number 14. After further editing, the bulletin evolved into Fleet Training Plan 219 (F.T.P. 219), which was dedicated solely to the purpose of charting the antisubmarine curriculum for the duration of the war. The training plan was further augmented with a publication entitled "Characteristics of Enemy Submarines," which was approved and published by the Commander in Chief, U.S. Fleet, on 22 January 1943. Containing the latest available information on enemy tactics and equipment, this work was widely distributed throughout the fleet as well.[140]

Baker was also responsible for introducing the British- designed "attack teacher" to the training curriculum. He obtained several of the devices from England and, with their permission, negotiated production contracts with General Electric, Sangamo, and Submarine Signal Company to build a series of "attack teachers" for the American Navy. They were soon placed at various locations, including Little Creek, Virginia. He also promoted close cooperation with experienced Royal Navy officers so that American personnel could profit from their successes. The program of instruction was demanding and required the participation of every available instructor. Eventually, Captain Baker moved his operation headquarters from Boston to Washington, D.C., in April 1942. Finally, on 3 February 1944, the unit was transferred to the Atlantic Fleet's headquarters in Norfolk, Virginia, under the Commander Fleet Operational Training Command.[141]

A faculty to man the various schools that grew out of the ASW training plan was drawn principally from civilian specialists with backgrounds in engineering, physics, higher mathematics, and teaching. The core faculty of this effort formed what became known as the Anti-Submarine Warfare Instructors School located at Boston Navy Yard. Before taking their positions throughout fleet training units, they were sent to Fleet Sound School at Key West. Following completion of their training, instructors from this school were soon able to teach basic and graduated ASW programs using attack trainers in the Fifth Naval District.[142]

Once adequate number of ASW-trained crewmen were in the training pipeline, consideration was given to training Navy officers with a specialty in antisubmarine warfare. As early as 20 July 1942, the subject was raised in a conference with Commander Destroyers, United States Atlantic Fleet. At first it was contemplated that these officers would comprise former civilian instructors, but it was soon discovered that the manpower pool from which selections might be made was not deep enough. Instead Baker chose to recruit officers from college midshipmen training programs. In late July 1942, Northwestern University sent the first class of future ASW-trained officers to Boston. Subsequent classes came from similar programs at Dartmouth and Princeton. They received further instruction at sound officers course at Key West before they were assigned to escort vessel duty. After successful completion of on-the-job-training, they received their orders to various commands through the Commander in Chief, United States Fleet. Within a year of its opening, the school had produced enough trained officer-instructors so that attention could be turned to enlisted specialty areas as well. By February 1944, both enlisted- and officer-level instructors were rotated for refresher training. The training units more than exceeded their goals, qualifying 150 attack teacher instructors and graduating 462 antisubmarine specialist officers by November 1944.[143]

Consideration was given to naval air forces as well. By 1944 an ASW indoctrination course for aviators was initiated with three full-time instructors. These classes convened for two-week sessions and focused on "convoys, sono-buoys, MAD (the magnetic airborne detector which locates the magnetic fields produced by a ship), bomb spacing and relative value of bombs, sono-buoy trapping and gambit tactics, and surface tactics." To augment classroom instruction, field trips were arranged to Submarine School, New London; the Radiation Laboratory, Massachusetts Institute of Technology; the Naval Air Station at South Weymouth, Massachusetts; the ASW Instructors School; and a ship to inspect ASW installations and equipment.[144]

Concurrent with the development of ASW training was the research and development spearheaded by the Anti-Submarine Development Detachment. The principal task of this unit was to identify and critically evaluate all new methods and weapons in antisubmarine warfare. Significant improvements had already been made in chemical recorders to register accurately the sinking times of depth charges and depth charge pistols to detonate the explosives from 300 feet to a range of 600 feet.

With the addition of the "R & D" detachment, research was particularly dedicated to the improvement of underwater sound equipment and ASW weaponry. An example of a successful effort in this area was the development of a radio sono-buoy for antisubmarine aircraft that had, at the beginning of the war, dropped from the priority list. Because of this concentrated focus on improving the ASW arsenal, an improved bombsight and a towed submersible target for use in training ASW aircraft were designed.[145]

As a direct result of this effort and the extraordinary number of new aircraft weapons and procedures, the Commander in Chief, United States Atlantic Fleet, commissioned the Aircraft Anti-Submarine Warfare Development Detachment, U.S. Atlantic Fleet, at the Naval Air Station, Quonset Point, Rhode Island. As outlined in 1943, its mission was to conduct experiments with airborne antisubmarine equipment and develop improved tactics for the accepted equipment, including attack procedures, convoy escort, and night tactics for aircraft assigned to ASW warfare. Furthermore, it was tasked with establishing a liaison with surface forces and "other agencies engaged in anti-submarine warfare development or research both within and outside the Navy." By the end of 1943, the Anti-Submarine Development Detachment was divided into two divisions, Aircraft Division (formerly the Aircraft ASW Development Detachment) and the Surface Craft Division. The detachment also served as a clearinghouse for international intelligence gathered on U-boat tactics with regular correspondence from Naval Attaches in London, Ottawa, Cairo and other British ASW sources.[146]

So that the entire ASW training program would be subordinate to one type command dedicated only to training, the Anti-Submarine Warfare Unit was placed under the control of the Commander, Operational Training Command, U.S. Atlantic Fleet, on 19 July 1943. Once the Unit was established as Task Group 23.11 of Task Group 23, it was charged with the following responsibilities: command, supervision, and administration of all the facilities attached to the unit, including the ASW Instructors School, and responsibility for the control and coordination of the methods of ASW instruction employed at all surface craft training centers where the Commander, Fleet Operational Training Command, had cognizance. However the critical concern of Task Group 23 was to "accomplish the most effective training and indoctrination of all ASW specialists and attack teacher instructors ordered to the Unit and to insure that the methods and procedures of ASW instruction at all surface craft training centers are adequate and in strict accord with the latest approved standards, to the end that all personnel and units will be fully ready for active operations against enemy submarines upon completion of their training periods." This mission was underscored by the continued inspection of all ASW training sites by Task Group personnel, with deficiencies brought readily to standard. Giving ASW training his highest priority, the Atlantic Fleet Training Commander had the unit moved to his offices in Norfolk, Virginia, on 3 February 1944 so that even a closer liaison might be maintained.[147]

Combined with the Anti-submarine Development Detachment, a formidable training, research, and development program had been initiated and established within the space of one year. The enlisted crew and officers, together with a wide array of new equipment and tactics, were now ready to test their classroom skills in real ASW operations.

# CHAPTER 6

## THE TABLES TURNED
## (THE SINKING OF U-BOATS
## U-85, U-352, U-701, AND U-521)

"The captain of a submarine is a king. He is the boss and nobody is there to tell him what to do. He has the order to do his best—to shoot as many ships as possible—no difference, warships or otherwise."

Captain Hellmut Rathke, commanding officer of *U-521*, thus summarized the arrogance and confidence of the German submarine navy in 1942. Despite this feeling of omnipotence, with Great Britain nearly choked off from the world by the sea and the United States now fighting a two-ocean war, the tide of war was about to swing, albeit against the odds, in America's favor.

The real turning point in the battle to defend the Fifth Naval District came as early as April 1942. Beginning that month and continuing over the next three and one-half months, only 35 vessels were attacked by U-boats, whereas attacks on the enemy increased to 153. With more Navy ships on patrol and cargo ships traveling in convoys, the German U-boat's so-called "Happy Time" was over.[148] The spring of 1942 saw the realization of Grand Admiral Doenitz's fear that if the U-boats did not attack with sufficient strength, America would be able to build up its antisubmarine defenses to intolerable levels.

The Fifth Naval District's ASW full fighting capability was finally tested in April 1942 when the *U-85* was sunk in district waters. This was the first German U-boat sunk off the East Coast during World War II. Its significance, however, was greater than that. The supposition that the U-boat was indestructible was at last disproved. The spell cast by their successes in early 1942 when they had made three kills a day, or one every eight hours, had finally been broken!

During its last cruise, the *U-85* had been precariously close to the Virginia coast, with Virginia Beach clearly within periscope range. At one point the *U-85* lay in wait on the bottom of the ocean just off the Virginia Capes. She preferred more plentiful game, however, and sailed south to Cape Hatteras on the Outer Banks of North Carolina. The destination of the U-boat had earned the name "torpedo junction" because of the large number of successful enemy attacks there.[149] While deployed in this favorite of all killing zones, the *U-85* encountered the USS *Roper*, one of the World War I-vintage destroyers that had been recommissioned for ASW duties. The *Roper* had been overhauled and given both radar and sonar for its service in the Key West Sound School. She was more than a match for a U-boat, and she proved it on 14 April 1942.

A few minutes after midnight, with the Bodie Island Lighthouse just off its starboard side, *Roper's* sonar picked up the sound of "rapidly turning propellers," which coincided with an initial contact made by radar. When *Roper* closed to a range of 2,100 yards, a wake was seen similar to one made by a small Coast Guard cutter moving at high speed. Captain H. W. Howe guessed that it might be a U-boat. Taking no chances, he sounded general quarters and the crew manned the machine guns, the 3-inch guns, the torpedo launchers, and the depth charge batteries. *Roper* closed, increasing her speed from 18 to 20 knots. The target began to change course repeatedly, attempting to evade its pursuer. Captain Howe kept the ship slightly starboard of the target in case of torpedoes. His precaution paid off when the U-boat fired from its single, stern tube. With *Roper* closing to just 700 yards, the track of the torpedo passed just to her port side.

With the *Roper* within 300 yards, the U-boat turned hard to starboard, attempting to use its sharper turning radius to evade the Americans. As she began her turn, the *Roper's* 24-inch searchlight illuminated the U-boat's light-colored hull for the first time. Immediately, the American gun crews opened fire with their machine guns. Some of the German submariners, running to man their deck gun, were quickly cut down, while others sought cover behind the conning tower. In the beginning of battle some of the *Roper's* ammunition misfired. However, a shell from the number five 3-inch gun made a direct hit amidships, just below *U-85's* waterline. The U-boat began to sink with approximately 40 men still climbing out of the vessel or already over the side. Despite the ferocity of combat the majority of *U-85's* crew still maintained discipline and was able to scuttle their submarine seconds before it disappeared stern first below the surface. Captain Howe ignored the floundering men in the water, making no immediate effort to rescue them. The safety of his ship and crew was his first concern. Knowing that U-boats often operated in pairs, he realized that his ship could be targeted by another German who could now easily zero in on *Roper's* illuminated searchlight. The sonar did indeed pick up another contact. Whether it was the sinking *U-85* or a second U-boat is not known. Not taking any chances, Captain Howe ordered a barrage of eleven 300-pound depth charges. The Germans stood no chance in the water from the concussion of the powerful explosions.

The following morning, a number of dead German crewmen were found floating in the general area. Five bodies had been recovered when, at 0850, a "sharp echo" was picked up at a range of 2,700 yards. The *Roper* dropped four more charges, which brought up a huge air bubble followed by a slick of fresh oil. By 0932, the last of the U-boat casualties were aboard *Roper*. Naval Intelligence officers had the grim duty of conducting a preliminary search through the dead crewmen's uniforms for information. Following a photograph session, two bodies, so horribly mangled that nothing could be discerned from them, were cast over the side.

A total of 29 enemy dead were then transferred that afternoon to the Navy tugboat USS *Sciota*. As Navy photos show, this was a gruesome task. The bodies were stacked on a tarp placed on the tug's deck. Blood could be seen clearly draining from the mound and coalesced into small puddles.[150] The "War Record of the Fifth Naval District" states that "the reason for the death of the 29 was given as drowning." The Navy Intelligence report, however, clearly indicates that the deaths were caused by concussion. The dead crewmen and their effects were further examined at the Naval Operating Base in Norfolk, Virginia. A detailed report on their condition indicated that the skin of the bodies was discolored from broken capillaries just under the skin. For example, the report on body number four, Erich Degenkolb, described his face as "blue, ears purple, and his neck and chest as spotted pink."[151] As water conducts sound better than air, these men did not have to be near the explosions to be killed. The shock wave, or concussion, was more than enough to rupture organs in their bodies.[152]

On 15 April 1942, at 2000, they were laid to rest in the National Cemetery, Hampton, Virginia. Services were read by both a Catholic and a Protestant chaplain. A saluting party of 24 seamen fired three volleys, followed by the playing of taps.[153] To disarm any potential protest by local citizens, the Navy reported that they were burying merchant seamen who had been killed in the current sinkings and whose corpses had washed up on the shore or were picked up at sea.[154]

Other successes against the U-boats followed the sinking of the *U-85*. On 9 May 1942, the *U-352* was sunk by the Coast Guard Cutter *Icarus* under the command of Lieutenant Maurice P. Jester, approximately 25 miles southeast of Beaufort Inlet, North Carolina. The crew of the *Icarus* picked up the still unidentified *U-352* on their sonar, which was estimated at 100 yards ahead. They immediately pursued the target. Moments after the chase began, a torpedo exploded approximately 200 yards off the *Icarus's* port aft quarter. Like the *U-85*, the *U-352* had the confidence to fire a torpedo at their pursuer. *U-352*'s torpedo was probably riding too close to the surface and "porpoised," or rose out of the water, throwing off its guidance system. The torpedo then plummeted to the bottom where it detonated. The *Icarus* immediately laid down several patterns of depth charges, which forced the *U-352* to surface. Now with the Germans easily in range, the *Icarus* opened fire with her machine guns and 3-inch guns, devastating the doomed *U-352*. The hapless U-boat crew quickly abandoned their stricken ship just minutes before she sank. At the same time Captain Jester radioed to shore, "Spotted sub, sank same."

Unlike *Roper's* deadly attack on *U-85*, *Icarus* did not follow up with additional depth charges as no secondary target was detected. Consequently, 33 German sailors survived and were taken aboard the *Icarus*, including the captain, Hellmut Rathke, who recalled the harrowing moments of his capture.[155] "We were swimming and seven of my men were shot down as they tried to swim from the *Icarus*," he said. "The ship passed and one American cried from the megaphone, 'Damn Germans, Go to hell!' Ok, we said, 'Go to hell!' Then the boat left. Two and a half hours later the boat returned and I heard a 'Mita, mita, mita' (Rathke's interpretation of machine gun fire). And we were not swimming away now—not at all, just shot!

"Before we entered the ship, I told my men while in the water to be silent about all military dates. You can tell of yourself and your family but not a word about anything else. All of them took these instructions very well. Nobody told anything—and this was in the report from the Pentagon. It was the fault of the Americans for leaving me together with my people aboard the *Icarus*. After that I understood they said never more (referring here to a change in American handling of German Navy POWs). You have to separate the officers and men![156]

"We were delighted after we got tables of breads and the next day chicken and coffee and all things—like the Americans—every day the same nourishment as the sailors. This was the first good experience I say. We had nothing against the United States Navy except the fact that they shot down swimming people."[157] To dispel any doubt about being shot at while swimming, Rathke repeated his story regarding the moment he and his crew abandoned ship.

"When they [the crew] left the boat in this action, the turret was just five centimeters out of the water. So I left first—just stood in the water hanging and ordering my men, 'Come up, come up, come up.' Then just as one man was coming out, they shot him—'Bang!' After that they began firing in the water at the swimming people. Yes, that is a fact!" To further underscore the veracity of the story, Rathke added that after the war, he received a written account from one of the crew of the *Icarus*, an ordinary seaman. "Just one sailor boy wrote me a letter and in it he said that he cried, 'Stop firing, stop firing! They are survivors!' These things are forgotten and done with now—we are friends together and I don't like to bring all these things from the bottom."[158]

*The U-701*, having surfaced approximately 30 miles east of Cape Hatteras, had a far more desperate time when it was discovered on 7 July 1942 by Second Lieutenant Harry J. Kane of the 296th Bombardment Squadron on patrol in his Lockhead Hudson. Seeing the plane, the *U-701* submerged, but Kane promptly attacked, dropping three 350-pound depth bombs, two of which were on target.

Captain Horst Degen described what the attack was like on his U-boat. "At 1:00 we went up, looked through the periscope. No noises in the microphones, the sky clear of airplanes; a sunny day with some clouds up high, water depth at 90 meters. A little eastward the bottom of the sea would go down till 1,000 meters within a few miles. By sheer luck we went on a west course instead of east when emerging for air-renewal. 'Blow all tanks.' 'Diesels full speed ahead.' The skipper and three good reliable look-outs were on the bridge in case some enemy would show up! The ship dashed forward in a fresh breeze which was soaked into the rooms. No ships around, no airplanes! Far in the West against the distant shore we could make out the funnel and mastheads of a wreck we had already marked on our charts. About five minutes later the engineer-officer gave sign from the control room that the ship is all right with fresh air. 'Let's go down again. Take her down!!' The diesels stopped with a hissing noise from the opened tanks. *U-701* began to settle through the surface. Two lookouts already had jumped down the hatch. Now the third man jumped towards the hatch and cried, 'Airplane 200 degrees-coming in from port-aft!!!' As he fell down the hatch the skipper had already taken a terrified look in that direction—he saw--a bomber dashing down from under a cloud."[159]

"The *U-701* managed her best diving, in no time she was at 30 meters depth. The crew was given a short word of what was to happen the next moment, it was silent within the sub, only the electro-motors which ran at full speed gave their singing melody. The drowsy lookout, who had obviously seen the bomber too late, received a reprimand, which he accepted with a nod of his head. Everyone stared at the instruments as the ship went deeper, but all this took only seconds. At 35 meters it happened! Two roaring crashes with tremendous vibrations, two depth charges had hit us at the stern and ripped the aft-hull to pieces. An overwhelming flood of water came with terrible speed through the door from the aft. 'Blow all tanks,' but that could not work anymore. The tanks were blown but the ship went down due to the heavy water that tumbled in from the engine rooms. The instruments showed 60 meters when with a slight bounce our badly damaged submarine was thrown to the bottom of the ocean! The water inside rose by the second. Within half a minute the whole ship was filled to the hatches where the inner air was pressed against the ceiling by the outer pressure that came through a terrible opening aft with 6 atmospheres. The lights were all out with only the little emergency lamps left burning. The ship had settled on an even keel listing to starboard about 25 degrees."[160]

Kane later described what he saw immediately after the attack: When we turned to look back and check what happened, we could see a terrific bubbling, I mean big bubbles, the size of a house, coming up out of the water. We saw some men come up in the center of where these bubbles were, and at that time we knew we had sunk a submarine because they might try to fool us by sending up oil and stuff like that, but they wouldn't send up men![161]

Degen continued to describe the desperate situation within *U-701*: There was no connection (communications) with the other rooms. The doors were flooded. There was only 30 centimeters of air below the ceiling and a terrible heat due to the sudden pressure. I remember yelling, 'Everyone get out of here, abandon ship!'"[162]

Meanwhile, Degen accompanied by his navigator and helmsman climbed up the ladder into the conning tower. The terrific heat that was building within *U-701* followed the three crewmen up the hatchway. Suddenly there was chaos as Degen recalled:

"I opened the main hatch and with a sudden lift I was thrown out of the hatch as the compressed air now got a vent to explode. With strong swimming motions I at last reached the surface and found myself amidst a bubbling soda-fountain. The sea was pretty rough for a swimmer but that did not mean so much at the beginning. And then the way was free for all![163]

"Every three or four seconds another man popped up beside the swimmers and pretty soon we were 16 men. And these all rose from a depth of 50 meters. But why didn't the others come up? Nobody will ever know. The men in the engine room may have been killed by the bomb hits, but there were some more men in the central control room. They did not manage to get out of the ship. But what about the men in the fore ship? We had no connection with them."[164]

Once on the surface Degen and his survivors found out quickly how inadequately they had prepared.

"Unfortunately the 16 men had only managed to bring five life belts with them and when we made the first assembly, we took the five life belts together for a raft so that everybody could hold on fairly good."[165]

Fortunately for the *U-701*, Kane remained overhead as the Germans crafted a makeshift raft.

"Above our heads circling around, the pilots opened their windows and waved at us. Suddenly we saw two life belts being dropped by the pilots. One of them fell very close by and the other went out of reach. We were thankful anyway![166]

"So we began to struggle along. Sixteen men in sport trunks. Swimming on six life belts in a warm, very salty, rough sea. It was July 7, 1942, about 1300 hours. We were sure to be rescued because the American pilot had given us a friendly wave and a life belt. He would go to the next base and call for a ship.[167]

"I passed the order among the men not to talk and not to ask questions because we had to save strength for the swim. But soon two men who could not swim swallowed the wrong way and were terribly suffocated by their coughing. Nobody could help them, although we all tried to hold them. The poor boys drowned half an hour later. We went on swimming that afternoon and tried to keep up good spirits and a hopeful mood."[168]

At this point, Degen recalled that their hope of rescue by the Americans helped maintain their spirits and will to survive.

"We thought it would be quite something for the Americans to get hold of German submariners. Thinking of these facts and this situation we got much at ease as far as a rescue was concerned. We talked it over how lucky we had been by going toward the coast and not eastward toward the open ocean with a depth of 1,000 meters (3,000 feet). All of us would have been lost immediately had we not hit the bottom at 60 meters (180 feet) depth."[169]

But as the day grew longer, some of the crew became less optimistic.

"As the afternoon went on, some of the boys got a little afraid of what would happen if no rescuers came until dusk. They were persuaded to keep still and hold on. But later on two more men who were pretty badly hurt by the explosion (a fractured shin and a severe head wound caused by a falling steel loudspeaker) went down due to exhaustion. Two petty officers, not being content with just drifting along without any effort to help ourselves, left the group by swimming in a westward direction [by the sun] in order to reach one of those wrecked ships we had always been seeing the weeks before. We have never seen those two men again for it was senseless to really swim toward the coast as the beach was about 30 miles away. The men were also swimming against the Gulf current that has a speed of two m.p.h.[170]

"We could only wait and see, saving our physical and psychological strengths. Just before sunset, we could see a large convoy of big freighters and tankers passing by at a distance of about four miles, too far to be seen for only our heads showed out of the rippled waves. Several airplanes passed high above.[171]

"Night came. The water was pretty warm, the sea calmed a little and our task was just to hold on to the raft of inflated six life belts. We were about twelve men left for some more had given up due to a severe hopelessness which they could not overcome although the men with stronger characters did their best to encourage the weak. The night went on pretty fast as we might have been sleeping and dozing which may seem to have been impossible, but it is the truth.[172]

"Next morning, July 8, a coast guard speedboat approached from the north. As far as we could see, she would have hit our position, but suddenly she zig-zagged away some degrees and passed in a distance of about 1,000 meters or approximately 3,000 feet. We waved our arms and yelled but it was all in vain. We could see the crew on the bridge but unfortunately the sea was so rough again that the speedboat could not see us. We became even more distressed as we were pretty sure that they were looking for us along with the airplanes. This feeling of desolation did not fail to have a bad influence on us. After a few hours this day, more of our crewmen gave up.[173]

"A tremendous thirst and hunger also began to give us terrible pain. The warm, salty water being swallowed now and then completed the nasty work of the burning sun which was pounding on us. Oil, which was oozing out of tankers torpedoed by our subs, began to smear and stain our faces. We had to hold our noses in order to protect it from the smacking waves which otherwise would have irritated our inner-nose and throat. But we could not prevent it and a terrible burning was the result.[174]

"During the day nothing happened as far as any rescue was concerned. But by nightfall there were only seven men left in our group. Agony came over us. We talked a little about things we would never have again. The murderous thirst gave us hallucinations. We chatted about drinking beer. We thought that beer would be a wonderful thing right now—and we wondered why we didn't drink more beer in the foregone life!!"[175]

Just before Degen and the remaining men grew too weak to hold on any longer, some relief literally floated by.

"On this afternoon we had at least a very little refreshment. First there came a yellow lemon drifting along. We tore it in two halves and each of the men could suck from that sour fruit. It burned like hell in our throats but it also gave a little stimulus! Next there came a coconut drifting in its hard, wooden shell. We managed to bore the two holes open with a safety pin that I pulled from my sport-trunks (the rubber string had grown too wide and Degen had tightened it with a safety pin earlier), then each of us could take a sip of the milk which was rotten and tasted awful, but we did not mind. Then we tried to break the hard shell of the nut and succeeded in doing so by hammering it onto the little steel bottle from one of the inflated life belts (compressed air container with a screw-shaped handle for letting the air go into the belt). At last the shell broke away and we got to the white meat inside. There was a piece for each of the men which was chewed in a hurry!"[176]

In their condition, as Degen recalled, even a few scraps of coconut could be dangerous for the remnants of his crew.

"But then came a bad surprise! With our stuffed noses, which were swollen inside and blocking our air, we were forced to breathe through the open mouth. But now that our mouths were full of coconut crumbs together with salt water, we were given to a dramatic coughing. Almost all of us were nearly suffocated because those coconut crumbs were taken into our lungs. A really dreadful situation—one can hardly imagine!"[177]

A sudden drop in the sea water temperature, according to Degen, left them close to shock as they continued to contend with extreme hunger and fatigue.

"And so ended July 8 at last. The sea had now grown calm like a still lake in the woods. But soon it became very cool as we either drifted much more to the north or crossed a cold current. We kept busy and warm by clinching with our neighbor and rubbing each other's legs. But the hallucinations grew worse during the night and some of the boys tried to make a getaway from the group.[178]

"We caught them and held them fast. One of them dreamed and talked dizzily and stole away about four times. It had then become foggy and at last we could not find him. He had managed to escape into the misty night. No use calling for him as he was lost.[179]

"In the early dawn of the next day, July 9, 1942, there were now only four men left. All the others had gone or were dead—at least we thought so because we were the only survivors of our group that escaped through the tower hatch.[180]

"The navigator, the first control room petty officer, the second radio petty officer and I were now all drifting in the calm ocean. In spite of all the help we had been giving to each other, we could not prevent the others from being drowned.[181]

"When the sun rose again it was with a murderous heat. Hallucinations started again, and now with the upcoming day they at last became almost unconscious. We dreamed away while hanging onto the life belts while a terrible sun beat down on our heads. The raft had untangled and I had drifted away from the other three who were no longer able to care for another."[182]

Suddenly the appearance of a shadow from overhead gave Degen's men some hope that they might still survive.

"At noon, the three sleepy and gazing men beheld above them a big balloon! It was a blimp of the United States Coast Guard which was on submarine patrol. The blimp did not sight a sub out in this moment but three nearly unconscious survivors of *U-701*! At a height of 30 meters (90 feet), the blimp stood still, a cabin door opened, and a second pilot shouted to the men, 'Who are you?' The men answered back, 'From a German submarine.' Minutes later the cabin door opened again and a big, inflated rubber raft was thrown onto the water. The three men found it hard work climbing into the raft but they succeeded.[183]

"When they had settled down in the raft, hardly aware they were rescued at last, a window on the blimp opened and a man shouted, 'Over there, one man!'[184]

"The three boys in the raft got the idea and paddled with their hands over the raft's side towards the other man. He was hanging onto a half-inflated life belt; his face just above the water's surface.."[185]

As the American airmen watched from their blimp, the three Germans rescued their captain, Horst Degen, who was just moments away from drowning.

"At first they called for me in vain, then they grabbed me and got me into the rubber boat. The rescue came at the last minute before I too would be a victim of this terrible exposure and exhaustion. When the four of us were in the boat, the blimp threw down cases with food, bread, some juice cans, and a rubber bag full of water. Some blankets gave us protection from the terrible sunshine which we could no longer stand. After having given us all the help we needed, the blimp took off and disappeared."[186]

Degen recalled that about three hours after the blimp left, a seaplane landed at 1400, approximately 50 meters away from their location.

"We saw the men of that seaplane standing on the wings and lighting their cigarettes. We four men lay listless in our boat and observed the Americans, each side waiting for a move from the other. Since the seaplane could not move without starting its motors just to taxi over to us, they waited for us to come paddling over to the plane.[187]

"Well, we were 'tough soldiers,' and being almost out of our minds from the terrible exposure of the last 50 hours, we obviously did not want to paddle ourselves into captivity as prisoners of war. Uncle Sam's pilots on that plane smiled at us and finally gave us encouragement by waving their hands to come over. And so we did![188]

"Two strong men grabbed each of us and lifted us swiftly into the plane. After that the rubber boat was taken inside. Without much talk, we were politely ushered to the stern of the plane where four bunks were ready for us to lay down. And now came the big surprise.[189]

"When we tumbled down the way to our bunks there were three other places occupied by exhausted men. They were three men out of the other group that had come from the *U-701*'s front room. Thus far we had not known they escaped!

"Later we learned that when the bombs hit, all the men in the fore ship gathered in the front room. They had closed the partition doors, although the water flooded throughout the ship, and then they opened the front hatch that was used to shove the torpedoes inside the ship. It was hard work under the heat and pressure; but finally the hatch was open (normally it was heavily blocked) and the group escaped the ship half an hour later.

"About 20 men came out to the surface. They also had to swim 50 hours, two days and nights. Only three of them were rescued; one diesel mechanic and two torpedo mechanics. "The seaplane took off and went to Norfolk, Virginia, where we were taken to the Naval Hospital for a three-day recovery. They took good care of the seven of us who were the only survivors of the *U-701*'s 46-man crew. But we were very depressed. We had drifted and swum about 90 sea miles or about 170 kilometers. And that was the reason the United States Coast Guard ships and airplanes did not find us. They obviously did not think of the strong current (Gulf Stream) that took us northwards.

"The bomber crew that knocked *U-701* out paid us a visit in the hospital (Here Degen apparently refers to the Navy's hospital facility in Norfolk, Virginia, as he was later moved to the Portsmouth Naval Hospital). They congratulated us for being rescued and assured us that they had immediately sent for help, but they did not find us soon enough to prevent most of our boys from being drowned. I can remember the name of the American pilot was Harry Kane!"[190]

When he [Kane] entered the hospital room, Degen, who was seated at a table, stood up, saluted, and said, "Congratulations, Good Attack!"[191]

As courteous as they might have been, the survivors of the *U-701* were good at keeping secrets. During their internment they never admitted mining the sea lanes near Virginia Beach the month before. In fact, the post mortem prepared by the Navy on the sinking of the *U-701* reported that the U-boat did not carry mines.[192]

Another U-boat, the *U-521*, was attacked on 2 June 1943 by the Navy patrol craft PC-563, piloted by Captain Walter T. Flynn. At 1235, approximately 142 miles east-northeast of Cape Henry, the PC-565's sonar operator picked up the submerged *U-521*, under the command of Lieutenant Commander Klaus Heinz Bargsten. Within a range of 1,600 yards, Flynn ordered general quarters. When they closed within 100 yards of the target, they dropped a pattern of depth charges. The *U-521* was rocked and damaged by the blast, forcing the crew to surface. Meanwhile Bargsten scrambled into the conning tower. The PC's crew opened fire with their heavy machine guns and proceeded at 15 knots to ram the U-boat.

With his U-boat severely damaged, including a destroyed diving rudder, Bargsten decided the situation was hopeless. With the PC bearing down on them again, he yelled down the hatch, "Flood all tanks, abandon ship!" The U-boat plunged, however, with unexpected swiftness, trapping the entire crew inside. Only Bargsten, by virtue of being in the conning tower, survived. As the ship was drawn from beneath him he saw water swirling into the open hatch, drowning out the shouts and screams of his dying crew. Freeing himself from his doomed U-boat, Bargsten was later picked up by the PC.

Despite the U-boat commander's statement that his ship had been sunk, the PC continued to patrol the area. At 1338 they found the grim evidence confirming the success of their attack as part of a human torso was found floating among the wreckage. As the U-boat sank in 1,700 fathoms, it was never positively located; however, it is undoubtedly there, rusting on the bottom like an iron coffin containing the remains of her entire crew except the captain.[193]

# CHAPTER 7

## *JOINT EFFORT*
## *(ARMY AND NAVY COOPERATION:*
## *THE HECP & UNDERWATER DEFENSES)*

Early and highly successful attacks on German U-boats within the Fifth Naval District and adjacent areas were mounting as the war progressed, but something far more substantial than mere chance was needed ultimately to turn back the "Wolf Packs." Those in the strategy centers deserve great credit for bringing together the Army and Navy into a joint operation against the U-boats. Before the United States officially entered the war, both the Army and the Navy realized their cooperation was crucial to the protection of the Virginia Capes and the Chesapeake Bay. Neither the Army with its ground forces nor the Navy with its fleet could repel an all-out enemy offensive alone. Together, they would have to protect the sea lanes and shipping channels in the area with an effective warning system, as well as take the fight to the Germans.

On 22 April 1941, the Local Joint Planning Committee drew up plans for an Army and Navy Harbor Entrance Command Post (HECP) to be built by the Army at Fort Story. While the command post was under construction, the Local Joint Planning Committee decided to establish the HECP in the U.S. Weather Bureau building at Fort Story.[194] On 30 June 1941, the HECP was commissioned and put into operation under the command of Commander E.F. Clement, USN. The Army and Navy jointly occupied an office in the building with watch officers from both services. Together, they gathered information for their respective military commands from a variety of surface and air patrol craft, as well as the Virginia pilots who operated nearby. By this time, the approaches to the Chesapeake Bay were finally under a joint command.[195] This operation coordinated both the Harbor Defense and Inshore Patrol Forces. The Harbor Defense Commander and the Inshore

Patrol Commander both received "real-time" information from the HECP, which enabled them to respond quickly as the situation warranted.[196]

The HECP remained in the U.S. Weather Bureau Building until the following summer of 1942. With a permanent, underground facility at Fort Story now completed, the HECP moved by stages into its new home. In early 1943, the facility was enlarged to accommodate an emergency center for the Fifth Naval District Commandant and the Navy's command operations. Known as "Battle Station Three," this expansion included an exact replica of the Joint Operations Center located at the Naval Operating Base, Norfolk, Virginia. If the Joint Operations Center were destroyed by an enemy attack, this alternate command post would be ready.[197]

In 1943, the HECP reached its highest state of development. By this time it was also the joint command post of the Harbor Defense Commander and the Approach and Entrance Force Commander. Throughout the war, both Army and Navy personnel manned the HECP 24 hours a day. The Army ran its own operations room, which enabled it to coordinate control of the harbor defenses along with the joint control of the port entrance. Navy personnel operated an adjoining Navy Operations Room. The Navy's intelligence officers, who served as field agents for the Fifth Naval District, were also stationed there. The Army and the Navy each had approximately 100 enlisted men assigned at headquarters. They consisted of "observers, radar operators and maintenance men, signalmen, radiomen, and teletype, and telephone operators, with necessary assisting and supervisory personnel."[198]

HECP had six types of formidable weapons at its disposal. The first of these was the Army mines. From Cape Henry to Cape Charles, 59 ground-controlled mines had been placed to form an outer mine field. Four more groups of similar mines formed a secondary defense line across Thimble Shoals channel at the entrance to Hampton Roads.[199] The use of Navy mines had been abandoned following a revision of the Army and Navy Underwater Defense System in November 1942.[200]

The second level of HECP's defense network was the installation of Army and Navy hydrophones. Newly developed, hydrophones served as underwater listening devices which enabled an operator to clearly detect and identify the propellers of an approaching ship. The Army had seven hydrophones equally spaced across the entrance of the Chesapeake Bay from Cape Henry to Cape Charles. These were positioned in front of the outer mine field mentioned earlier. The Army hydrophones and mines were both operated from Army casemates. The Navy, meanwhile, placed its own hydrophones approximately 5,000 yards east of the Army's outer mine field and hydrophones. The Navy's 14 hydrophones were controlled, and their signals evaluated, in the Navy Operating Room at HECP.

The third component of the HECP plan was the operation of three Navy magnetic loops. These consisted of underwater cables that detected the magnetic field produced by a passing ship. The Navy loops were installed just east of the Navy hydrophones, thus forming the first defense perimeter of the Chesapeake Bay. The loops closely paralleled the hydrophones and were laid in three sections of roughly equal length stretching from Cape Henry to Cape Charles. Until late 1943, only the southern section, near Cape Henry, and the midsection were in place. The northern section consisted at that time of a Navy mine field which was later replaced by the northern loop.

The fourth barrier against enemy penetration was radar, with the HECP controlling both surveillance and fire control systems. Surveillance-type radar operated by the Navy's patrol craft as well as the Army's command posts at Forts Story and Monroe gave a picture of all surface craft in the region. The Army radar swept an area covering its artillery's field of fire and beyond. Each of the Army's 6-inch batteries at Forts Monroe, John Custis, and Story was equipped with fire control radar. Each of these radar sets could be operated in an emergency from the Army's Operating Room in the HECP.

The fifth layer of this defense program was Navy patrols operating from the Little Creek Base, monitored by the Navy Watch Officer. In addition to those maintained by the examination vessel and the Inner and Outer Guards, patrols were also conducted in the approaches to the Chesapeake Bay and given the colorful code names "Nude North and South, Sold, Jake and Fair." These patrols were augmented as the situation demanded. They were expected to serve both as a defensive and as an offensive deterrent.

The sixth and final defense was the Navy airplanes. These aircraft were used by the HECP for additional patrols to investigate incidents, and to aid the Harbor Defense Commander.[201]

Having such forces available enabled the HECP to protect the Bay and the maritime traffic in the area. Some of the major operations at the HECP for the Army and Navy included gathering and properly distributing intelligence data, operating and maintaining military communication channels, controlling mines and access of the port, firing warning shots on vessels recklessly off course, and giving protection to convoys.[202]

Working closely with the HECP at Fort Story was a similar operation called the HECP Number Two, located at Fort Monroe in the Groupment Command Post. Directed by the Army's Groupment Commander, the HECP

Number Two operated as an independent station directing traffic in and out of Hampton Roads. The Army and Navy had a similar close working relationship with HECP Number Two. The post also maintained contact with the Joint Operations Center at Norfolk. This program meshed well with the Navy's duties of operating the inner patrols, maintaining the nets across the entrance to Hampton Roads, and operating the minefield gate.

# CHAPTER 8

## *THE EYES AND THE EARS*
## *(THE ROLE OF NAVY*
## *INTELLIGENCE OPERATIONS)*

A key factor in the battle against U-boats in the Fifth Naval District was the availability of useful information gathered by the Operational Intelligence Unit of the District Intelligence Office. This operation had three interrelated activities that included coastal information collection, ASW analysis, and operational intelligence activities. Of these, the coastal information was the backbone of the intelligence effort, as it called for painstaking collection, evaluation, and dissemination of information to various intelligence departments. Such work was complex and detailed, involving the establishment of an entire network of contacts, informants, and observers. Work in this area began long before the war in anticipation of eventual hostilities.

ASW intelligence personnel organized a method of sending information on enemy U-boat movements in and around the Fifth Naval District to all available forces by installing a plot room in the Coastal Information Office. This enabled the courses of U-boats to be tracked with continuous updates from sightings. The courses of all friendly vessels in the district were also plotted for their own protection.

Operational intelligence distribution involved timely evaluation of collected information and its circulation to all friendly vessels in the region. Such information could furnish warnings to merchant ships and pinpoint targets for patrol craft. Every effort was made to collect complete information before distribution, thus greatly reducing the chances that a patrol craft might mistakenly fire on a merchant ship or allow a U-boat to slip by.

To cover all operational needs, intelligence officers were placed in each section base and air station. They not only gave information on friendly and enemy activity to outgoing pilots and skippers, but also received information from inbound mariners, making them a vital part of the information collection process.

The number of sources used by Operational Intelligence was staggering in diversity. Anyone who had any contact with the area was a potential source of information. Typical sources included public and private citizens who flew aircraft, sailed the seas, or operated radio communications, and those who visually monitored the area, such as Army Watch Officers. As mentioned earlier, most of the vessels fishing in Fifth Naval District waters were equipped with radios to transmit information on any U-boat sighting, making them another important contributor to the growing success of the Operational Intelligence Unit.[203]

Robert Hasler, current president of the Hasler Steamship Company, Norfolk, Virginia, recalled the days when, as an ensign, he joined Navy intelligence in the Fifth Naval District.

"I started as an ensign in January 1942 after graduating from Fishburne Military School and some military training. I had just started work in this company for my father when I heard that the commanding officer of Naval Intelligence, a Captain Gass, was looking for personnel who had any experience in merchant ships. There were four or five of us—that's all we had. That was sufficient as long as we didn't have to work all night long."[204]

Hasler recalled that the intelligence effort went into full swing immediately after Pearl Harbor and there was little time for training. "Soon after reporting to headquarters, they sent me to Notre Dame for about six weeks. But it wasn't geared to intelligence but rather an officers' training school. After that they sent me to one month of intelligence training in Washington, D.C.[205]

"My job along with three or four other officers was to board every vessel that came into the port of Hampton Roads. And during those interviews, the first thing we would ask crew members was, 'Did you see anything suspicious?' If the person being interviewed could tell us something, we were then required to take down the exact location. And some of those we talked to could remember exactly where they saw something, however the majority never saw anything that resembled a U-boat. You have to remember also that on the rare occasion that a ship did see something strange, they could not as merchant ships report it immediately as they would have to then break radio silence, giving away their position to a U-boat.[206]

"After a ship arrived in Norfolk, we would board and ask the captain if he or any of the crew saw anything suspicious—lights, or even a periscope. If they saw something, we'd ask them if they had plotted it on their charts and if they had marked it, we would ask them to let us have the chart. Then we would take their chart back to our second floor offices at headquarters and have it analyzed. After that we would return to the ship with replacement charts. By that point, the original charts with the information on them were on their way by air to Washington or anywhere else where they could be of some value.[207]

"Our main job was of course to meet ships as they arrived at the piers. If they went to anchor instead, which quite a lot of them did, we would take a Navy or privately-owned launch from Newport News or right outside the Naval Base. If the captain of a particular vessel didn't speak English, somehow we always managed to find someone to interpret for us. However the vast majority of captains could speak enough English for our questions."[208]

Hasler then described a typical day on the job gathering intelligence in the Fifth Naval District during 1942.

"We would always start at the pilot's office and the tugboat company and check what had come into the port and what went where. Then we would divide the list of expected arrivals— 'You take this one, and I'll take this one.' Then we would figure how many to take depending on how many were in anchorage. And then we would start the interview process that I mentioned earlier.[209]

"Along with the charts, we also had the power to review a ship's log books. If they saw something strange out there, it's going to be mentioned in the log with the time, date, and position of the sighting. If that corresponded to the chart, then we just might be on to something. And just like the charts, we would ask to borrow the log so that a copy could be made, and then it was returned. Again, sometimes we had to get interpreters to translate some of the citations. In a log citation, you might get something like this: 'Yes, we sighted a periscope.' But so often the citation would not give you any indication on whether it was an American, Allied, or German. So we had to go back to our own deployment schedules at that point to see who was supposed to be where. But we were seldom told in this case whether the sighting was American or German.[210]

"We also interviewed Virginia pilots regularly and of course local fishermen, but survivors were our most important source of information. The main thing here was to greet them when they finally got to shore and make sure they were in good shape. On rare occasions we would go over to the Naval Hospital in Portsmouth after the survivor received some medical attention. Then we would ask them questions about whether the submarine surfaced or not; and if it surfaced—did they fire guns at you, or did they try to pick you up and bring you aboard as a prisoner—generally questions like that. What we were really trying to pin down of course was the exact time and location of the attack and anything else that might help us track the submarine. We tried to keep any real incidents out of the press."[211]

At this point, Hasler recalled the gruesome story about *U-85* and the final destination of her crew.

"There was one incident where a German U-boat off Eastern Shore fired a torpedo at a tug towing two coal barges. The word got back to the air forces and they went out there and found the submarine and they bombed and sunk it. That submarine must have been hard up for targets to fire at a tug and a couple of barges![212]

"At any rate, I remember going down to headquarters the following morning when Captain Gass said, 'I've got a job for you. Go down and take the Little Creek ferry to Kiptopeke. An army truck will be there waiting for you and I want you to escort that army truck back over the ferry and go over to the Navy Base.'[213]

"Once we got the truck to the base, we were ordered to take it over a little bridge and across to a warehouse. By then my curiosity was up and I asked the captain what was in the truck. He said, 'Bodies!' I asked, 'Bodies of what?' He said, 'German bodies!' They had blown up this submarine (*U-85*). The submarine had apparently split open and the bodies came up. The captain also told me that if anyone asked what was in the truck, to deny knowing anything." [214]

Hasler stated that his office did not conduct a search of the bodies, but "others did." "They laid them out," he said, "still in their uniforms. Some got souvenirs of their buttons. I think it took about three or four days for their preparation. I believe they were buried in a plot at Forest Lawn in Norfolk and not over in the military cemetery at Hampton. They also removed their identification cards for their rank and names for the files."[215]

When asked why there was so much secrecy around the dead German crew, Hasler admitted he did not know. "The funny part was I remember all the ice around all these bodies. Water was dripping out the back of the truck. People would come up and ask what in the world do you have in that truck and I would say, 'Just a truckload of fish!' My theory is that we simply did not want to alert people that Germans were operating right off our coast!"[216]

On occasion, Hasler and other intelligence officers would frequent various officers' clubs in the district to "listen in" on conversations. "We would sit around at night and wait to hear some officer who had taken too many drinks start spouting off about what he saw and did. Then we would have to go over and warn them not to spout off about something they shouldn't be talking about, and if it got out of control, then we would call the shore patrol, but that didn't happen very often."[217]

Captain Hellmut Rathke, *U-352*'s commanding officer, offered another unique perspective on how U.S. and Allied intelligence officers collected information.

"During my interrogation by American officers, they asked me if I had a daughter. Then after I said yes, they would ask me when was her birthday and what happened at her birthday party. I never spoke about this because if I say I took part in the birthday, then you know I couldn't have left at that point, so with discretion I didn't answer. When I didn't, they laughed.[218]

"And then they asked about my entering the Navy first in April 1930 as midshipman—so I must have been in Hamburg by an excursion of my command and had a dance in this bar of so-and-so with this girl. She was their girl and they said they knew through her all the dates of my career.[219]

"We also had a good man in the Navy school. He was a captain, married to an English lady, and he was the teacher of English language for all the years I was there. He knew all the crews before me exactly and all these dates were passed on to the English Navy. Nobody had any idea that he was an informer—a spy!"[220]

By the time Rathke and his crew were captured by the *Icarus*, Allied intelligence gathering was well established. Rathke recalled that he was not asked any technical questions about his submarine during interrogation. "No questions and no answers concerning how we operated, because by then they knew all things. They knew all technical dates and data. They knew all because they would tell me things and my ears grew longer and longer and then I knew that they had good knowledge. But no questions and no answers!"[221]

Despite Rathke's obvious respect for Allied intelligence, he credited USCG *Icarus's* discovery of his submarine purely to chance.

"Just when I reached the American coast, about one day before, I met a German submarine commanded by Albert Schnee and he called to me, 'What are you looking for here? Here is nothing to do, go back, be patient and keep your shirt on and leave, here is nothing to do.'[222]

"But I had instructions to stay there. So I remained. And then the first ship I saw was the *Icarus*. I had dived earlier and now was on the surface patrolling when suddenly I saw the mast getting bigger and bigger.

"Well that's a good target I decided, so I shot two torpedoes. The year 1942 marked a bad time for German torpedoes as they had been disastrous, but I didn't know why. Somebody said that it was sabotage planned by the

English. But I don't know.[223]

"The torpedoes exploded just 200 meters from the *Icarus*. A good target! My people were very, very good. And this statement I can make after four years of prison with them. They had been good all the time. Then I looked out of the periscope—4 o'clock in the afternoon, quiet water, looked again, and they had stopped. For the American side, they did what was right—they attacked."[224]

Rathke considered it a "miracle" that *Icarus* was not sunk after he fired his two bow torpedoes at almost pointblank range and at a perfect angle. However the misfired torpedoes alerted the crew of the *Icarus* and gave away Rathke's location as well. "Before that, they had not heard us," admitted Rathke. "We made no noises at all. If we had not fired, they would have never known we were there. But then they stopped and looked—which was good luck for the *Icarus*. She was my first target and I did what I thought I should—and that's how I take it."[225]

Another fascinating source of information was found in flotsam, which spoke volumes in unwritten words. Simple pieces of wood washed up on a beach or snagged floating by a fishing boat could no longer be ignored, as they might carry a registration number of a vessel listed as missing. Empty lifeboats and life preservers were often found by fishermen and beachcombers and furnished grim evidence of a ship's identity that was before only "presumed" sunk. Occasionally, a more macabre means of identification appeared on the beaches in the form of U-boat victims. For example, ten days after the 500-ton, HMS *Bedfordshire* was sunk on 11 May 1942, two waterlogged corpses washed ashore on the Outer Banks of North Carolina. They were later identified as members of the crew. Several days later, two more members of the crew were found. Unfortunately, the identities of these men were never known.[226]

On 4 June 1942, the crew of the trawler *Sue Lawson* presented to the District Intelligence Office a large piece of metal that was caught in its net while fishing near Winter Quarter Shoals Whistle Buoy. The metal fragment turned out to be a German electric torpedo motor, which was one of the most advanced of its kind at the time. What fouled up a potentially good day of fishing for the *Sue Lawson* became a tremendously valuable "catch" for Naval intelligence.[227]

Besides offering invaluable information, flotsam sometimes had good salvage value. Some of the material collected in intelligence-gathering operations was later resold—sweep cables, sonar-buoys, and copper cable.[228]

However, despite the best efforts of military intelligence, U-boats managed to capitalize greatly on their tactical advantage during the early days. Operational intelligence obviously sought to remove this advantage by developing, analyzing, and updating a tactical record of local U-boat operations. Once the information was judged accurate enough, it was distributed through official channels. Included in the data distributed on a U-boat's potential locations were the tactics employed by the enemy. For example, it was discovered that a surfaced U-boat on 11 January 1942 had successfully simulated the flashing light of the Hatteras lightship, which lured the American collier SS *Venure* in close for the kill.[229] The U-boat commander waited for the lightship to be taken into port, and simply took its place. The *Venure's* captain was tragically ignorant of this trick, which led to the loss of his ship. Another trademark enemy tactic was the way U-boat commanders liked to stalk a ship, waiting to strike when the night watch was changed, as it took a while for the eyes of the replacements to adjust to night vision.

U-boat tactics naturally changed throughout the war, giving Operational Intelligence a challenge to keep ahead of their methods. However, in spite of the creativity of the enemy, U.S. intelligence did a masterful job keeping everyone informed. For example, in the fall of 1943 they reported that aircraft on patrol should be more careful in their attacks on U-boats, as the enemy was no longer crash diving at the sight of an airplane but instead remaining on the surface and defending themselves with antiaircraft guns.[230]

Mine warfare remained a deadly threat and high on the interest list of district intelligence. Accurate accounts of all friendly minefields as well as reports on all potential enemy sightings were warranted to keep Allied vessels out of harm's way. Military intelligence trained approximately 500 observers who monitored the harbor channels for "friendly" mines that had "walked," in addition to the enemy ones that disappeared. These observers "scored" many finds, enabling countermine warfare teams to quickly remove the deadly obstructions.

When *U-701* mined the entrance to the Chesapeake Bay in September 1942, the investigation conducted by Operational Intelligence uncovered some disturbing facts. During August and September, intelligence officers found papers aboard Spanish, Portuguese, Greek, and Swiss neutrals warning them to take an alternate route through the Virginia Capes, avoiding a specific area of the swept channel where mines were later found. Fortunately, no American ships fell victim to one of these mines before they were removed.[231] However, the following cases offer strong evidence that the international rules governing neutral shipping had probably been violated.

The War Diary of the Fifth Naval District records that "the Greek steamship *Helene Kulukundis*, boarded at Baltimore on September 14, (1942), carried routing instructions which differed to a considerable degree from those issued by the United Nations. The instructions, dated July 10, and issued to the *Kulukundis* by the Swiss Legation in Portugal, directed her to proceed from Bermuda to a point somewhat northwest of the Chesapeake Lightship Buoy and from there straight into Cape Henry. The ship was specifically warned against following the swept-channel."

If this was the only example of "safe sailing" instructions, it could have been logged as pure coincidence, but according to the War Diary, "identical instructions were issued by the Swiss on July 20 to the SS *Calanda*," on a similar voyage to Baltimore. Also listed in the "suspicious" column were the SS *Monte Mulhacen* and the MV *Kassos*. Both arrived in Baltimore on September 29 with Swiss instructions dated September 8 in Lisbon that were identical to those of the *Kulukundis*.

One of the more substantial examples of possible collusion between neutral shipping and German/Italian sources is the case of the Swiss *Saentis*, which according to the War Diary "reached Baltimore on September 7 from Genoa, with instructions from the Italians, dated at Genoa, August 9, and also Swiss instructions, dated at Genoa, August 17." The instructions were identical to the location of the lightship buoy and firmly directed that the ship sail no farther south of a line from Chesapeake Lightship to Cape Henry.

Navy officials argued that "all United Nations routing instructions direct vessels to follow the regular swept-channel into Cape Henry by way of Chesapeake Lightship and Buoy 2CB. These are issued in Lisbon by the British Consular Shipping Office and are available to all neutral ships who wish them. Therefore, it is strongly indicated that neutral nations had been notified by the Germans of mines to be laid near Buoy 2CB."[232]

The Fifth Naval District Intelligence Office had little trouble determining that these incidents were clear violations of neutrality. In a Coastal Information Section Report released on September 30, 1942, Naval intelligence concluded that "a neutral nation, supposedly with no first-hand information of the approaches to a belligerent harbor, would undertake to issue routing instructions for the entrance to the harbor in direct contravention to the instructions issued by nations charged with keeping a channel into such harbor open and free of mines, must certainly be communicating with enemy agents."[233]

While the Fifth Naval District's ASW effort was being organized, the number of ships sunk in the area, and off the Chesapeake Bay, grew dramatically. Many ships were sunk in shallow water and constituted a hazard to navigation. Consequently, the Operational Intelligence Unit had the duty of informing traffic in the area of these potential hazards. These wrecks also created headaches for patrol craft, as they were difficult to distinguish from a submerged U-boat sitting on the bottom. Many depth charges were wasted in needless attacks on wrecks, including the Civil War ironclad USS *Monitor* off Cape Hatteras.

Lieutenant Junior Grade H. R. Wood, the District Wreck Officer, was placed in charge of the "collection, evaluation, and dissemination of wreck data in the Fifth Naval District."[234] Under his direction, a survey of the wrecks in the water of the Fifth Naval District within the 100-fathom curve was conducted. This survey was performed with the use of the USCG *Gentian*, which began operations on 17 July 1943. During the summer months of 1943 and 1944, the survey continued. When the operation was completed on 30 September 1944, 418 wreck positions had been investigated, with a total of 65 positively identified. Although this information came late in the war, it still furnished invaluable data years after the war to maritime traffic.[235]

The Operational Intelligence Unit was also involved in some "cloak and dagger" operations to identify and capture all possible enemy collaborators. Soon after the war began, rumors circulated throughout the district that collaborators were in the area collecting food, water, oil, and information for the U-boats. The possibility that enemy agents had infiltrated the region seemed plausible to the Operational Intelligence Unit, as the area's geography and history lent themselves to infiltrators, bootleggers and smugglers. Again the Department of Naval Intelligence depended on local observers to record and report "suspicious activities" and suspected collaborations.

Fishermen in Morehead City, North Carolina, were reported to have discussed openly how they were either willingly or unwillingly stopped by a U-boat and relieved of their supplies. One report from the Fourth Naval District revealed information from a "reliable" source who described how large amounts of oil were stored in the Lower Delaware Bay, New Jersey, for refueling submarines.[236] It also described a U-boat hideout and repair facility located somewhere in the same vicinity or farther south near Norfolk, Virginia. Many of the so-called reports were simply rumors and were quickly dismissed as such. Some, however, did warrant further investigation, and were taken as serious potential threats by the Operational Intelligence Unit.

The District Intelligence Office was assigned the task first of preventing espionage, and second of verifying or disproving suspicious reports. The progress of its inquiries was routinely reported to the Coastal Information Section. Assigned the extensive monitoring of all ships entering and leaving the district, intelligence employed five methods to accomplish this daunting task: 1) Reports were made to the Coastal Information Section by the locktenders on the Chesapeake and Albemarle Canal and the Dismal Swamp Canal; 2) Intelligence officers boarded every small vessel, including fishing boats, both entering and leaving the Chesapeake Bay; 3) Daily Coast Guard reports were prepared on all craft entering or leaving all inlets along the coast; 4) Informants were to monitor all points where a boat could enter or leave that was not monitored by the Coast Guard; 5) All outgoing craft had to give their expected operating area, which was later checked by patrol craft and airplanes. If a ship failed to radio in a deviation from its course, it was subject to disciplinary action, such as the revocation of its operator's license.

All of the small craft in the district were screened, and those considered posing a danger were placed on a "suspicious small craft list." This list was constantly updated, which was no minor task in Hampton Roads. At one time, the list numbered over 200, but by 1943 it was reduced to less than a dozen due to "negative investigations, gas rationing, and in a few cases, revocation of operating license."[237]

The office's second objective, however—verifying or disproving reports on suspected collaborators—proved more difficult. Intelligence officers could never track down the source of a rumor. If they asked a waterman for the source of a rumor, the typical response was that the informant had just "heard" it. Unfortunately, talk about U-boats and local collaborators made good gossip, and some of it was picked up by journalists and printed as fact in the newspapers. Regardless of the story's origin, an agent was assigned to conduct a full investigation. One such story appeared in a North Carolina newspaper and described a chance encounter between a fishing boat and a submarine. After the investigation was complete, it was found to be groundless. As a result, most papers in the Fifth Naval District agreed not to publish such stories in the future without first checking with Naval Intelligence for verification. Thereafter, the flood of rumors was greatly reduced.

Other reports of collaborators on shore attempting to communicate with the enemy at sea were equally difficult to confirm. The Coastal Information Section chased down literally hundreds of stories that were disproved. On rare occasions, though, there were legitimate reports of communication from shore to U-boat. For example, communication through visual signals was confirmed in several districts. One was confirmed in the Fifth Naval District when a series of flashes were seen originating from the coast to seaward. Upon investigation, it was found that the number of flashes corresponded exactly with the number of ships in a convoy awaiting departure.[238] Most of the reports of flashing lights, however, were dismissed as shooting stars, lighted buoys, and running lights on small vessels bobbing up and down on the waves.[239]

Collaborators were also suspected of communicating with the enemy by radio. Most of these "suspicious" radio signals, however, were explained as nonhostile. In fact, no tangible results were ever uncovered in the Fifth Naval District. Most signals were attributed to such things as garbled Army and Navy transmissions, radio beacons, Allied naval vessels using foreign codes, enemy propaganda, and even enemy operational transmissions. A principal culprit behind the reports of enemy radio transmissions was the occasional presence of the mobile Federal Communications Commission (FCC) monitoring station. Typically, these were large trucks or vans loaded with electronic gear. During the war, the Federal Bureau of Investigation raided one of these FCC units, thinking it was transmitting messages to the enemy.[240]

It was also feared that enemy agents were clandestinely dropped off in the Fifth Naval District. Even though Navy intelligence has no irrefutable evidence that enemy agents ever came ashore here during the war, foot patrols were maintained nonetheless along the shore. Both the Army and the Coast Guard assigned personnel to these patrols, which monitored all of the beaches and the harbors. In late 1943, with more Army personnel being transferred overseas, the Coast Guard, in agreement with the Navy, took over all the beach patrols except for Virginia Beach, which was under patrol by units from the Coast Guard and Army at Fort Story. Personnel at various lifesaving stations along the coast were also ordered to keep their eyes seaward and report any questionable observations to the nearest authority. Coastal areas like those surrounding Forts Eustis, Monroe, and Story were still patrolled by Army personnel. Controls were quickly tightened during the first year of the war, making it highly unlikely that an enemy landing ever occurred.[241] The rumor persists that after a depth charge attack on a suspected U-boat contact, debris was uncovered that included ticket stubs from a movie theater in Norfolk. Supposedly several German spies must have been aboard. This story has remained in the rumor column and has never been substantiated.

Perhaps the crowning achievement of the Navy's Operational Intelligence Unit was its direct contribution to the sinking of several U-boats in Fifth Naval District waters. As earlier described, the USS *Roper* sank the first U-boat, the *U-85*, off Nags Head on 14 April 1942. The *Roper* did not just stumble on the *U-85*; rather, accurate intelligence reports guided it to target. The crew of the *Roper* received all of the acclaim in the press for this first kill. However, it was the intelligence operatives, behind the scenes, who made it possible. Indeed, it was the Intelligence Unit that doggedly pursued the movements of the then-unidentified *U-85* for two weeks straight. Reports from aircraft and ships at sea that spotted the U-boat continually updated its location. The *U-85* was one of three U-boats known to be operating in the Fifth Naval District at this time. However, it was discovered to be remaining on station in a small area just off Nags Head. The last report on its location came on 13 April from Captain Quinn of the fishing trawler *Sea Romer*. Participating as an observer, Captain Quinn radioed his sighting to the Naval Operating Base at Norfolk. His report corresponded well with the Navy's estimation of the U-boat's position. The *Roper* was ordered to the location with the dispatch, "Something suspicious due east of Currituck in 15 fathoms of water." In the early hours of the next day, the *Roper* was right on target and the U-boat was destroyed.[242]

That same year, Navy Intelligence aided in a similar fashion with the destruction of the *U-701* on 7 July by an Army A-29 bomber 37 miles east of Cape Hatteras. The captured Captain, Horst Degen, gave the Navy a description of his ship's activities in the Fifth Naval District that matched exactly with the times and locations estimated in operational intelligence reports. In fact, the Navy's Operation Intelligence Unit contributed to all of the hundreds of attacks made on enemy U-boats in the Fifth Naval District. Not all attacks were successful, but due to improved intelligence networking, the District's waters became a very dangerous place for future U-boat operations.

Alan Flanders presents Reinhard Hardegan a copy of *Guardian of the Capes*, a history of the Virginia pilots during WWII.

Reinhard Hardegan examines his original U.S. Tour Book that he had as a mid-shipman, and later used on his first patrol to American waters.

*Top*: Alan Flanders looks over the shoulder of Horst Degan as he explains his mission to the American coast. *Bottom*: Horst Degen, former commanding officer of *U-701*, studies a chart of the approaches to Chesapeake Bay where he successfully deployed mines during World War II

*Top*: Helmut Rathke points to some underwater photographs of his sunken U-boat, *U-352*. *Bottom*: Rathke, now retired from his civilian job, has taken up painting as a hobby.

*Top*: Helmut Rathke stands before a wall of memorabilia at his house. *Bottom*: (left to right) Alan Flanders, German Navy Flag Lieutenant and Helmut Rathke standing on the grounds of the German Naval Academy at Flensburg

Full View of the *U-995*, a type VII submarine on exhibit at Laboe, Germany. The Baltic Sea is in the background.

Russ Powell stands before *U-995* exhibit at Laboe, Germany.

Russ Powell points to the depth gauge in the control room aboard the *U-995*, a type VIIc submarine at Laboe, Germany.

John A. Fahey, former U.S. Navy Commander and board member of WHRO, stands before the Navy blimp he piloted on ASW duty.

*Top*: U.S. Navy Blimp on ASW patrol. The very sight of these flying leviathans gave comfort to the crews aboard the merchant ships under escort. *Bottom*: Flight deck of a Navy Blimp undergoing pre-flight checks prior to an ASW patrol

Joseph A. Kelly, former U.S.C.G. officer, stands watch during submarine patrol.

Robert Hasler, former Fifth Naval District Intelligence Officer.

Linwood Hudgins, U.S.C.G. retired, shows the swept channel leading into the Chesapeake Bay.

*Top*:  Linwood Hudgins points to his old command, the U.S.C.G. Buoy Tender *Orchid. Bottom*:  Coast Guard Buoy Tender *Orchid*

*Top*: U.S. Navy Patrol Craft serves as a picket ship during convoy duty. *Bottom*: Private yacht converted by the U.S. Navy for picket duty as part of the ASW effort.

Alan Flanders and Russ Powell (left to right) stand before the *U-995* at Laboe, Germany

# CHAPTER 9

## *ARMY AT SEA*

The Army and the Navy worked together to protect the Chesapeake Bay from the intrusion of U-boats or any other enemy vessels. In addition to cooperative efforts with the Navy such as the Harbor Entrance Control Post, the Army furnished formidable defenses with its complement of mines, forts, artillery, aircraft, and mobile forces.

U-boats were but one of the targets the Army defenses were prepared to meet. These defenses were also considered adequate to destroy or at least cripple any invasion force sent by the enemy. Even though the Army had substantial weapons, with a range of 25 miles, on Capes Charles and Henry, it had to be content with aiding the Navy in keeping U-boats out of the Bay. The Germans must have respected their weaponry, as no U-boat is believed to have entered the Bay itself, despite persistent claims by some writers to the contrary.

The Army was responsible for an area known as the Chesapeake Bay Sector, which was organized on 12 December 1942 according to guidelines in the *Joint Action of the Army and Navy*. The sector's parent organization was the Third Coast Artillery District, which was reorganized as part of the mobilization effort. The seaward boundary of the sector was the same as that of the Fifth Naval District. Consequently, the Army was responsible for the coast from the Maryland-Delaware boundary to the southern tip of Onslow County, North Carolina.[243] The Defensive Coastal Area around the entrance to the Chesapeake Bay was dictated in part by the range of the weapons at the Army's disposal. The outer limits of this area were determined by the radii of the projected arcs from the Fort Story batteries at Cape Henry (24,500 yards), and the Kiptopeke batteries at Cape Charles on Fisherman's Island (24,200 yards).[244]

Both the area around the Virginia Capes and the Chesapeake Bay were considered second only to New York in importance to the war effort by the Army. Defending this area also meant the Army was protecting the approaches to Washington, D.C., and Baltimore, Maryland, in addition to local military establishments. Should the Axis have taken over the region, it would have had the use of some of the best port facilities in the world, plus immediate access to some of the prime industrial centers of the country. Needless to say, an attack on Washington, D.C., would have been a tremendous psychological as well as strategic defeat for the United States.

As U.S. participation in the war became increasingly certain, plans were hurriedly made for the Army's role in defending the environs of the Chesapeake Bay and adjacent waters. Labeled the Army's "Operating Defense Plan," it was given final approval by the Commanding General, First Army, of the Northeastern Theater, on 8 July 1941. Under this plan, the area commander was given the task of defending the sector from attacks from the sea, land, and air. This involved coordination with Army aircraft from Langley Field. In addition, artillery units located at the surrounding forts, along with those on mobile platforms, were employed. The Army was also expected to furnish antiaircraft defense, covering such potential targets as government buildings, Langley Field, the Norfolk Naval Base, Norfolk Naval Shipyard, Newport News Shipbuilding, and the ammunition and fuel depots located in Nansemond, Norfolk, and Yorktown. The Army was also ordered to work closely with the Navy in joint operation of the Harbor Entrance Control Post. Army mines were also used to augment the already established underwater defenses protecting the entrances to the Chesapeake Bay, and Hampton Roads.[245]

The man responsible for the successful execution of these plans was Brigadier General Rollin L. Tilton, who took command of the Chesapeake Bay's harbor defenses on 9 November 1940 after serving a month earlier as commander of the 6th Artillery at San Francisco. Following his services in the Chesapeake Bay Sector during the war, he served as Inspector General of the Army Ground Forces and headed the War Department Seacoast Defense Armament Board.[246]

Tilton divided his command into two groups consisting of the outer defenses, protecting the entrance to the Chesapeake Bay, and the inner defenses, guarding the entrance of Hampton Roads and the surrounding inner area of the Chesapeake Bay. The outer defenses consisted of Fort Story at Cape Henry, and Fort John Custis at Cape Charles. Fort Story had ten batteries plus control over 46 groups of mines guarding the entrance of the bay. The batteries included the following:

| | |
|---|---|
| Battery Ketcham | 2 - 16" guns |
| Battery 121 | 2 - 16" guns |
| Battery Pennington | 2 - 16" Howitzers |
| Battery Walke | 2 - 16" Howitzers |
| Battery Worcester | 2 - 6" guns |
| Battery Cramer | 2 - 6" guns |
| Battery 226 | 2 - 6" guns |
| Examination Battery | 2 - 3" guns |
| Battery AMTB No. 21 | 2 - 90mm guns |
| Battery AMTB No. 22 | 2 - 90mm guns[247] |

Originally, Fort John Custis, located near Kiptopeke on Cape Charles and Fisherman's Island, was known as Fort Winslow. It was renamed Fort Custis in February 1942, with the name later expanded to John Custis in October to avoid confusion with Fort Eustis, which was not part of the sector's defenses.[248] Fort John Custis had control of the remaining 13 groups of mines guarding the entrance to the bay in addition to the following five batteries:

| | |
|---|---|
| Battery Winslow | 2 - 16" guns |
| Battery 123 | 2 - 16" guns (canceled) |
| Battery 227 | 2 - 6" guns |
| Battery 228 | 2 - 6" guns |
| Battery AMTB No. 24 | 2 - 90mm guns[249] |

The inner defenses consisted of Fort Wool and Fort Monroe. Fort Wool was located on a small, artificially built island at the entrance to Hampton Roads known as the Rip Raps. Fort Wool had three batteries:

| | |
|---|---|
| Battery Gates | 2 - 6" guns |
| Battery Hindman | 2 - 3" guns |
| Battery Lee | 4 - 3" guns[250] |

In addition to Fort Wool, there was the much larger Fort Monroe, which not only had eight batteries but controlled four groups of mines at the entrance to Hampton Roads. The batteries included the following:

| | |
|---|---|
| Battery 124 | 2 - 16" guns (canceled) |
| Battery Parrott | 2 - 12" disappearing guns (disarmed) |
| Battery De Russey | 2 - 12" disappearing guns (disarmed) |
| Battery Anderson | 4 - 12" mortars (disarmed) |

| | |
|---|---|
| Battery Ruggles | 4 - 12" mortars (disarmed) |
| Battery Church | 2 - 10" disappearing guns (disarmed) |
| Battery Montgomery | 2 - 6" guns |
| Battery AMTB No. 23 | 2 - 90mm guns[251] |

As conditions warranted, continual manning and maintenance of some batteries were discontinued. In passing, one of the most unusual characteristics of coastal defensive artillery anywhere on the East Coast was implemented at Old Point Comfort. During exercises, crowds would gather either in their boats off shore or down the beach to watch disappearing cannons supported on a hydraulic framework recoil behind a massive concrete embankment and then return to view to resume firing. Upon firing, the concussion helped lower the weapon downward, causing it, much to the delight of the spectators, to simply disappear from view.

To augment the outer defenses of Fort Story and Fort John Custis, the Army decided an additional fortification was needed in the middle of the 12-mile entrance to the Chesapeake Bay. The Army came up with three possible plans. The first was to construct an artificial island on which a fort could be built. The second was to build a tower in the middle of the Bay entrance from which artillery could be placed and fired. The third was to anchor a huge hulk laden with artillery as another defensive measure.

The first two ideas were too lavish and expensive. However, the third was supported by the War Department and the Navy. The old gunboat *Annapolis* was acquired for this project, and preparations were made for her to be equipped with cannons and manned by coast artillery personnel. Although the project seemed reasonable in early 1942, support faded by 1943 as the Battle of the Atlantic began to shift to the Allies while the Fifth Naval District's ASW program was significantly improved. Consequently, the Navy withdrew support and the project was abandoned.[252] The necessity for further defense works was reduced by the modernization of the Army's arsenal on Fisherman's Island and Cape Henry. As a result, the "middle-ground" of the Bay entrance was more than adequately defended and now easily within range of the Army's guns.[253]

Tilton wasted no time establishing the coastal observation system on 24 March 1941. Well before Pearl Harbor, a permanently manned observation post was installed at Fort Story. There was strong suspicion that even without a declaration of war, the enemy might already be targeting the Chesapeake Bay Sector. The first permanent, 24-hour, harbor defense alert was established on 22 May 1941. Army guns in the outer and inner defense network, including the anti-aircraft guns, were readied. The vigilance of this alert was raised as the threat intensified. On 4 November 1941, secret orders were given to all Army commanders in the sector not only to maintain their surveillance and cooperation with the Navy, but to attack with lethal force any German or Italian forces that dared to enter the area.[254] On 7 December 1941, after word was received that Pearl Harbor had been attacked, the entire Chesapeake Bay Sector went on full alert status with every gun and station manned and troops ready to move if necessary. The sector was now in a wartime mode, which was made official on 12 December 1941, when General Order Number One formally placed it in operation.[255]

The alert status of the sector was gradually lessened as the perceivable threat to the region grew more remote. The efforts of the Army must have seemed anticlimactic, as the enemy never really challenged its defenses.

Toward the end of the war, Army operations within the sector were dramatically scaled down as a large number of soldiers were transferred to the West Coast for the Pacific campaign. By 1944, the sector was classified as virtually free from attack and required only a minimal defense force. Plans were even made to deactivate the sector and incorporate it into a new Southeastern Bay Sector, which extended from New York to Florida. Orders implementing this plan went into effect on 29 February of that same year. All the defenses in the area were removed, including the formidable artillery pieces that had been rendered obsolete by the increased range and accuracy of long-range rockets.

# CHAPTER 10

## *KILLER TEAMS*

One of the best offensive weapons against the U-boats was the airplane, the very sight of which would cause the U-boats to crash dive. With speed, maneuverability, and an array of advanced weaponry, the airplane proved itself a more than adequate adversary. As mentioned earlier, few ASW-equipped airplanes with trained crews were available at the start of the war. Consequently, the first air patrols were extremely limited. Like the Navy ships, many planes had been redirected to battle zones overseas in Europe and the Pacific, where the need was considered greater. When the war came, the Navy found it had virtually no bombers on the East Coast; it was left with Catalina seaplanes. Designed primarily for rescues and observations, they were also capable of attacking with a limited number of depth bombs. Multi-engine bombers, capable of longer ranges, were desperately needed to counter the U-boat threat.

The Navy recognized the seriousness of the situation and called on the Army for help in March 1942. The Army answered the need by giving Rear Admiral Andrews operational command of all Army Air Force units designated for use in protecting shipping. With that coordination of resources, an effective air defense was born. At this time, 83 Navy planes, 4 Navy blimps, and 84 Army planes were located at 18 different fields along the East Coast. Military planners knew that this number was inadequate. More airplanes were finally dedicated to the ASW effort, and by the end of July 1942, the Navy had a total of 178 planes and 7 blimps, augmented by 141 Army planes. These airplanes were stationed at 26 airfields that dotted the Atlantic coast of North and South America from Jacksonville to Argentina. Many of these were not just surveillance craft, but formidable war planes like the Army's A-29 bomber. An additional benefit at this time was the advent of training in antisubmarine air warfare and research by the

Seasearch Attack Development Unit at Langley Field, Virginia.[256]

To improve communications between the Army, the Navy, and the different air bases, an Antisubmarine Army Command was organized in October 1942 with Brigadier General Westside T. Larson in command. Under his administration, the ASW Air Command created two new air squadrons, the 25th, headquartered in New York, which served the Eastern Sea Frontier, and the 26th, headquartered in Miami, which served the Gulf area. The 25th Squadron reached full strength by 26 February. At this time, it had 124 Army planes, 174 Navy planes, and 17 Navy blimps, all available from 20 different bases located between New Brunswick, Maine, and Jacksonville, Florida. The 26th Squadron had 96 Navy planes and 62 Army planes based at 14 fields located between Banview River in Florida and the Grand Cayman Island in the Caribbean. Due to administrative problems, the Navy eventually assumed full control over the air defenses off the Atlantic, as the Army Antisubmarine Air Command was disbanded in 1 September 1943.[257]

During this period of development, the flying hours logged by Army and Navy aircraft in the Eastern Sea Frontier went from approximately 5,000 hours in January 1942 to a peak of approximately 25,000 hours in July 1942. In the first four months of 1942, aircraft attacks averaged about 12 per month, increasing to approximately 45 a month over the next five months, giving an average of about 30 attacks a month for the period. Approximately 20 percent of these attacks resulted in at least some damage to the U-boats, while about 2 percent resulted in the sinking, or at least the probable sinking, of a U-boat.[258]

Many of these air attacks were made in the Fifth Naval District. When airplanes were not covering a convoy, or attempting to locate and rescue survivors of a U-boat attack, they usually flew patrols hoping to catch the Germans on the surface. As described previously, an Army A-29 bomber caught the *U-701* on the surface and sank it. Other, similar attacks were made, of course, but not with the same conclusive end. However, air surveillance undoubtedly offered effective harassment, with many of the attacks inflicting damage resulting in the U-boat having to abort its mission.

In addition to the performance of the fixed-wing aircraft, the contribution of Navy blimps must not be overlooked. They served in many roles, such as patrols, search and rescues at sea, and escorts for convoys. Although their offensive capabilities were limited, the very presence of one of these flying behemoths hovering next to a convoy gave comfort and reassurance to the merchant seamen.

John Fahey, a Hampton Roads educator and board member of WHRO

Public Television, Norfolk, Virginia, was an airship pilot who participated in numerous missions along the coast of the Fifth Naval District. (Following the war, Fahey served as an intelligence officer in Berlin during the Cold War era.) He remembers well the role played by airships, which proved to be very versatile, functional, and well equipped to handle the missions assigned to them. The airships used by Fahey and others during the war were the K-Class manufactured by Goodyear. They had a capacity of 416,000 to 456,000 cubic feet of helium, but usually contained 425,000 cubic feet. They had a length of approximately 250 feet. More than 130 ships of this class, numbered from K-3 to K-135, were built during World War II.[259] Rather than being slow and cumbersome as their size and shape may imply, the airships proved to be very fast and agile.

"We had Pratt and Whitney engines. I don't recall the horsepower, but the average cruising speed was about 55 knots, and you could get up to 65 or 75 knots maximum. The props were like those of an airplane, the regular pull props," Fahey said.[260]

The airships flown by Fahey were referred to as "non-rigid," which means that they did not have a metal framework for internal support of the enormous bags containing the helium. "To help keep the air pressure inside, you had what we called ballonet with two on the bottom of the bag which allowed us to control the expansion of the helium. The whole airship is regulated or shaped by internal pressure. With one forward and one aft (ballonet) you could trim the airship. They were very useful for that. You could make the nose heavy by pumping more air in the aft ballonet for example. Their operation was very similar to a submarine's ballast tank," said Fahey.[261]

According to Fahey, the blimps carried some rather impressive firepower. "Fifty-caliber machine guns were assigned for our use with one per ship. . . located in front of the car (gondola). You have two pilot seats. And right down there below him is the bombardier seat with controls. And up above that (the pilot seats) . . . out front sitting over plexiglass, you would go through a hatch into a small bubble. You couldn't elevate the machine gun as it would hit the bags. We also had contact bombs underneath and depth charges attached to the sides. We carried . . . four depth charges. First we had depth charges up to 1943 and then after 1944, we had contact bombs and depth charges; and then in 1945, it was real secret, we had homing torpedoes. They had a range of two or three miles. You went out there to bomb anything that moved!"[262]

To enable the blimps to perform their ASW duties they had to have the best detection equipment available to track and pursue enemy U-boats. "We had sonar buoys of course. Even in '43, we had MAD (magnetic airborne detector, which detects magnetic anomalies produced by a ship). It had a range beneath the airship of 300 feet and that was well within the pressure depth of a German submarine. Then they increased the MAD range depth to 600 feet. The subs could not go down that far. Finally, I think at the end of the war, the subs were going down about 1,000 feet, and the MAD was developed to keep up. They could not escape MAD under the water. You flew 50 to 75 feet over the surface. The lower you were, the better the signal, so I would go as low to the surface as I could even though they recommended that we fly 100 feet above," recalled Fahey.[263]

Fahey described how sonar buoys were deployed from his airship. "First you would get a disappearing radar contact and then you hit that spot with a pattern of sonar buoys about 3,000 yards in radius around the target. You would drop around 8 to 12 sonar buoys. Next you would listen and find out where the sub was going. Of course, you would fly over the patterns (of sonar buoys) until you picked up a signal. You had graph-type paper, and that would give you a signal, like a W on the paper. Then you would develop a pattern and drop smoke floats on them. Once you got the smoke floats on target, you would see his track and you would go down and drop the depth charges and contact bombs and at the same time radio in with the information, especially the location. You had two radio men who had to send in a report immediately about a disappearing contact."[264]

The Navy was very interested in anything spotted by airship pilots. Navy intelligence officers briefed them prior to deployment and later debriefed them on their return. "We all hoped," recalled Fahey, "that we might have the opportunity to actually sink a U-boat, which could in those days earn you a Navy Cross."[265]

In addition to their detection equipment, the airships offered a stable observation platform. "The visibility is tremendous. We were all in plexiglass, so you had visibility in the front, back, and all over," said Fahey. With virtually unlimited range of visibility, the crews continually kept an eye out for the characteristic silhouette of a U-boat. In addition, they were able to take detailed photographs for Navy intelligence. "We had a K-20 camera, I know that well. I loved to use it. Hang out there by my toes and take pictures. I even photographed a dog on one of our (U.S.) submarines," remembers Fahey.[266]

The airship crews did receive training in how to detect, pursue, and attack German submarines but it was not extensive: "a little bit—but certainly not too much," said Fahey. "In fact," Fahey continued, "while I was serving in Blimp Squadron 15 in Georgia they decided to send us aboard our submarines. Not everybody went, but I went down to Key West, Florida, to observe our submarine commanders and how they would react to air attacks and so forth. So we would go down in the R-boats, which were small and leaky. They always told us that the moisture was condensation. You didn't want to get claustrophobia down in those things. But we would observe the captain on these training exercises as they took evasive action during different circumstances like an air attack. That was very interesting being down there in those submarines and then, later on, flying overhead and hoping to find Nazi submarines and contemplating what they might do."[267]

Flying in the role of ASW platforms, airships quickly established their value in suppressing U-boat operations and were deployed throughout the war. "We used to run patrols two or three hundred miles out and also escorted convoys that came down the shipping route. But the submarines (U-boats) didn't submerge that much, instead they had to surface and get into an attack angle, they just weren't fast underwater. They had to actually race ahead of a convoy to cut it off. So keeping them down was one of our greatest contributions to ASW. We used to deploy 10 to 20 airships a day off the East Coast, and then we deployed them off South America as well."[268]

Fahey was justifiably proud of their successful performance in convoy protection. "The airships escorted 89,000 ships during World War II and never was there one ship escorted by an airship lost. We did a lot of escort duty, sometimes escorting a single ship." Airships did their best to maintain continuous escorts of ships. Typically airships would meet a convoy en route along the coast relieving the airships that had been in escort. "Well, someone would pick them up and deliver them to us and then we would escort for 16 hours (or more) and hand them off again to another airship. We had bases from Massachusetts to Georgia...right on down the coast. After we deployed them off the coast of South America, all the north-south shipping lanes were covered. Now, out of escorting some 89,000 ships, I would say that we flew more patrols than escorts. However, I have been sent out to escort just a single ship before also. Never any troop ships, just a merchant ship. During this time, I was in Blimp Squadron 15 during the war and Airship Squadron One at Weeksville, North Carolina, after the war. We had ten airships in each squadron, at least ten airships."[269]

As blimps became the workhorses of the ASW air effort, Fahey recalled that they were deployed continuously, no matter what the conditions. "We went out there every day and flew in all weather, talk about being expendable! As far as weather was concerned, they would never do it today like we did. We would go daily. We never canceled because of weather. However, we almost lost our airship out there in a storm. I was the co-pilot on that one and the pilot asked to return to base. We could barely keep it in the air and were about 200 miles out. They came back and later chewed him (the pilot) out for asking HQ for a decision whether to turn back. Most of the ones we lost were in the weather. I was on the field in Lakehurst and watched one take off and then crash into a hangar because of the weather."[270]

Although Fahey flew airships in the Fifth Naval District, his home base was not located here. "My main base was in Glencoe, Georgia, located between Savannah, Georgia, and Jacksonville, Florida. After the war I was stationed at Elizabeth City, North Carolina. I used to come to Norfolk occasionally and up to Lakehurst, because the squadrons were moved around a bit. I was very familiar with this area during World War II." The dirigible base in the Fifth Naval District was located in Weeksville, near Elizabeth City. "We had one large hangar there with the 'orange peel' doors and then we had two (hangars) on the other side of the 'mattress' or runway."[271]

During the war, the airships usually carried a complement of six enlisted men during their long patrols or escort missions. "We had two radiomen (one would operate the radar) and two mechanics to operate the engines and two riggers, who would be responsible, for instance, if we made an attack. A rigger would arm the depth charges and release them; and now and then a rigger would fly the rudder. There are two controls, an elevator for controlling up and down and a rudder for controlling left and right. So then we had three pilots; one would navigate the entire time, and then the other would fly the elevator, and then we would rotate on the elevator while one rested because we would be out for many, many hours. A patrol could range up to 20 hours, that wouldn't be unusual. Some flights might be over 30 hours. Most of them were 15 or 16 hours. So two of the pilots would rotate on the elevator and the enlisted rigger would control the rudder. And during landing, all the pilots would be on the controls with one also acting as navigator."[272]

One airship from the Fifth Naval District proved that it was capable of making an attack on a U-boat. The non-rigid Navy airship K-7, commanded by Navy Lieutenant Commander G.E. Pierce, was escorting a convoy on 8 June, 1943, when, at 1020, a strong contact with a U-boat was made using the magnetic airborne detector (MAD). The contact was maintained with a bearing and location determined. At 1115, the K-7 dropped a depth charge over the location of the submerged U-boat which brought up a quantity of bubbles. At ten-minute intervals, two more depth charges were dropped, but without further results. It was obviously a good sign of success when their target stopped moving after the first attack.

Following the K-7's attack, two Navy planes, also furnishing air coverage for the convoy, assisted in the assault. They dropped two depth charges each, neither of which raised any telltale bubbles or wreckage. An hour later, two more Navy planes arrived, also attacking with two depth charges each, which likewise produced negative results. There was no further contact established with the U-boat. The Navy concluded that, "it is probable that slight damage was inflicted on a marauding submarine in this case."[273]

Although the K-7 did not sink the U-boat, its actions undoubtedly rattled the nerves of the stalking U-boat's crew. Regardless of the slight damage they may have caused, the U-boat was kept preoccupied with self-defense while the convoy sailed away unmolested. The Germans now knew they not only had to be aware of America's growing surface ASW arsenal, but also be mindful of attack from the air.

When German tactics changed, allowing U-boats to surface and use their antiaircraft guns, both Navy and Army planes were quickly modified to meet this threat with more forward firepower and additional armor. Regardless of how brave and inspired the U-boat crews were in defending against air attacks, this new tactic, on most occasions, proved to be more an act of desperation than tactical improvement. Even if they were not sunk, they often sustained enough damage to force them to return to base.[274]

On the other hand, a surfaced U-boat could be quite deadly with its antiaircraft guns. One U-boat made an impressive showing during the early morning hours of 7 August 1943. A PV-1 twin engine bomber, flying out of Floyd Bennett Field, Virginia, was on patrol approximately 200 miles east of Virginia's eastern shoreline when at 0730 it made radar contact with a U-boat only 12 miles away. The PV-1 pursued the contact and found it surfaced and stationary. The Germans did not seem to care that they had been found, which made the plane's crew question whether it was really an enemy submarine. After circling the U-boat once, they identified her as a German Type VII, with three men positioned around her aft antiaircraft gun. The PV-1 decided to make a run on the U-boat. The plane descended and began to strafe the target with its machine guns. Then, just as the plane dropped four depth bombs, the U-boat's antiaircraft guns roared back. The U-boat's gunner was on target and repeatedly hit the PV-1, blasting off its starboard engine and damaging the port one. Catching on fire, the plane filled with smoke, making it impossible for the crew to see if the detonating depth bombs did any damage. Even though the pilot had been severely wounded, he managed to keep the plane airborne for another 15 miles before making an emergency landing in rough seas. Two enlisted men in the tail section went down with the plane. As the battered plane quickly flooded and sank, the pilot, co-pilot, and radioman managed to escape. The strain, however, was too much for the wounded pilot. Bleeding badly, his strength ebbed as he struggled to remain afloat. After only a few minutes, he drowned. About two hours later, the co-pilot, Lieutenant Junior Grade Thomas J. Aylward, and radioman James A. Welch were rescued by a Navy PBM-P4 seaplane from the Norfolk Naval Air Station, which made a heroic landing in the churning sea to rescue them.

The drama of this daring U-boat was not yet over, as another PV-1 was dispatched to the same area. The U-boat was still on the surface. However, this time after spotting the plane, it decided to crash dive, discharging a few bursts from its guns. The U-boat had just submerged when the plane dropped four depth bombs over it, causing it to immediately resurface. The crew immediately manned their antiaircraft guns again. Just before the attack a PBM-3s seaplane from Elizabeth City also approached to attack. Following the PV-1's attack, the PBM began its own, but was hit several times from the U-boat's antiaircraft fire. The plane's bombs refused to drop, and its bow machine guns also jammed after firing only a few bursts. On a third pass the plane dropped all eight of its depth bombs. The U-boat again tried to submerge as the charges went off. This time sustaining some damage, the U-boat was once more forced to the surface. The U-boat appeared out of control, running wildly on the surface. Nevertheless, the Germans quickly manned their antiaircraft guns, firing at the PV-1, which followed the seaplane's attack with several strafing runs of its own. The U-boat continued to run out of control as the two planes circled above, their ammunition exhausted. After an hour, the crew regained control over their U-boat and immediately headed out to sea and submerged. The two planes then returned to their respective bases.

According to official records, it is possible that a second plane was shot down that day, possibly by the same U-boat. Another PV-1 from Floyd Bennett Field never returned from its patrol. No trace of the plane, or its crew was ever found, and the Navy later stated, "It is considered not unlikely that this plane, too, was shot down by the same enemy submarine, its entire crew sinking with her."[275]

Regardless of the punishing defense demonstrated by this U-boat, it did not get away undamaged. It was later learned that she had given up her original mission and returned to home base for repairs. Whatever mission the U-boat had off the East Coast was canceled due to the damage it received while remaining on the surface to fight it out.[276]

In conjunction with the use of the airplane, the Navy came up with a new antisubmarine tactic called the "Killer Team Doctrine." Developed by Rear Admiral Simons, Commandant of the Fifth Naval District, and initiated by the Navy in April of 1942, this doctrine called for the combined use of both airplanes and surface ships to track down enemy submarines. The plan required one destroyer and three aircraft, with at least one on station at all times. Their objective was to exhaust the U-boat's air supply, which had to be replenished on the surface every 24 hours.[277] Furthermore, the distance a submarine could run submerged was limited by its batteries, which could be exhausted, depending on the U-boat's speed. Again, the U-boat would be forced to surface and run on its diesels to recharge the batteries. Consequently, with these two limiting factors, a U-boat's probable surfacing area could be plotted within a 100-mile diameter. Also referred to as the "Ripple Method" by the Navy, this system depended on monitoring the wave of expanding contacts, like ripples, originating from the first U-boat encounter. Because of their inherent limitations, U-boats had to reappear within one of the expanding circles, which gave the "Killer Teams" a bull's-eye in which to bracket their target. The sinking of the *U-85*, as detailed earlier, was part of a Killer Team effort. The position of the *U-85* was pinpointed by aircraft on several occasions. This careful surveillance enabled the USS *Roper* to find the U-boat on the surface and sink it.[278] Innovations such as the Killer Teams helped to close the U-boats' "Open Season" in the Fifth Naval District.

Another deterrent that U-boats dreaded more than any other was the depth charge, the earliest ones being easily recognizable by their "ash-can" shape. The Mark 6 and 7 depth charges, with 300- and 600-pound charges respectively, were the only types in use when the war began. Of these, 35,586 had been delivered to the Navy by 30 November 1941. These charges were detonated with hydrostatic (water pressure) triggers. One disadvantage of these early charges was that they had a maximum depth setting of only 300 feet. This was fine for the U-boats of World War I, but not for the ones of World War II with their increased diving depths and thicker pressure hulls. Consequently, the triggering mechanisms were redesigned to allow settings to be made up to 600 feet. Further refinements produced a firing trigger adjustable to 1,000 feet. In addition, an improved deployment method came about with the introduction of the K-gun, a relatively accurate depth charge launcher that could place the charges in more controlled patterns, unlike its predecessor, the less accurate Y-gun launcher.[279]

The shape of the depth charges themselves was also improved. The streamlined Mark 9 depth charge was more accurate, as it could sink 100 feet in only 8.6 seconds. Furthermore, the charge was composed of Torpex, which was one and a half times as powerful as TNT.[280]

Before the war was over, depth charges were relegated to a secondary position. They were replaced by the more accurate and deadly "ahead-thrown" weapons, small rockets that could be launched directly onto a U-boat's suspected location. These projectiles sank very fast, detonating only if they hit the target. Without unnecessary explosions, it was easier for the sonar operator to maintain a fix on the U-boat. The Navy reports that these weapons were from 300 to 800 percent more effective than conventional depth charges.[281] Two such weapons, implemented by the Navy in 1943, were the "hedgehog" and the "mousetrap." The British-designed hedgehog employed a launcher containing six rows of spigots (long metal rods), of four each, on which the projectiles were placed. All 24 rocket projectiles were launched in a cluster to a targeted area. The mousetrap was a smaller American-designed version for use on ships that could not withstand the recoil or accommodate the size of the hedgehog. The mousetrap fired four to eight rocket projectiles at a time.[282]

Simultaneous development in other ASW-related areas, such as sound equipment, dramatically increased the accuracy of these weapons. Both America, with its "sonar," and England, with its "asdic," perfected echo-ranging. These systems employed a loud "ping" that echoed off the hull of a U-boat, betraying its presence.

Radar was also greatly improved. The first bulky model, with an enormous radar scanner resembling a huge vertically mounted bedspring, came into use in October 1941. By December, at least one ship in each convoy had one. The size of the individual radar units decreased while the range was improved. Eventually a smaller model, the SCR-517, was fitted into Army airplanes. Airborne ASW teams were further aided by the addition of the High Frequency Direction Finder, the HF/DF. Called "Huff-Duff" by Navy operators, the device led American pilots to U-boats by locating their radio transmissions.[283]

During the summer of 1942, because of innovations in weapons, support equipment, and the use of airplanes and surface craft, the U-boats were generally put on the defensive the moment they arrived on the East Coast. Much had changed since their arrival in 1942. America's new ASW plan no doubt must have startled those later U-boat captains and crews who had visions of the earlier successes garnered by the likes of Rheinhard Hardegan. Now stealth, instead of bold and brazen daytime surface attacks, became the U-boat tactic of necessity. Then the Germans answered with innovations of their own, such as the schnorkel, a breathing apparatus enabling the U-boats to run on their diesels at periscope depth while also drawing in fresh air for the cabin. However, U-boats equipped with these did not appear until 1944, and there were so few that they posed little threat to the East Coast.

The legacy of the German U-boat offensive against the East Coast of the United States was the Navy's resolve to build an antisubmarine warfare program. It took precious time and great sacrifice, but in the end, it played a pivotal role in turning the tide of the Battle of the Atlantic and dealing a crushing blow to the U-boat threat.

# CHAPTER 11

## *VICTORY*

The coordinated use of convoys, underwater defenses, air and sea patrols, Army fortifications, "Killer Teams," new weapons, and intelligence operations gave American forces the edge in the struggle to defend the Fifth Naval District. When the United States entered World War II, many of these defenses, although planned, had not been implemented. The result was an appalling loss in shipping as the U-boats operated with little resistance. Historians rightfully compare this initial slaughter to the attack on Pearl Harbor, and as for death and destruction, it was worse. And just like Pearl Harbor, there was in the beginning a failure to heed warnings from overseas intelligence that an attack like "Operation Drumbeat" was imminent.

The following charts (Figures 5A, 5B, and 5C) summarize with a solid line U-boat activity in the Fifth Naval District, and, with a broken line, the attacks on them. The chart illustrates a week-by-week reporting of this activity for all of 1942. In January, there is a sharp peak during the third week as the first wave of U-boats attacked during operation *Paukenschlag*. In February, activity subsided when many of the U-boats withdrew to their home bases for fuel and torpedoes. The U-boats returned to the East Coast with heavy activity in March, especially during the third week, when they sank 13 ships. Because there were few United States ships for patrols and district convoys were just forming, the U-boats operated with only minimal resistance. This situation soon changed; U-boat successes began to decline during the last week in March 1942. This continued, with a rise only in June, which resulted from the use of mines by the *U-701*. In July, only three vessels were attacked, which were the last of that year.[285] Appendix A shows that U-boat attacks were restricted to only three in 1943 and only one in 1944.

The chart also shows attacks on U-boats, which paralleled those on shipping. The maturation of the Fifth Naval District's ASW program is clearly obvious by April as the number of attacks on U-boats exceeded those on shipping. Attacks on U-boats continued to exceed the number of enemy attacks for the duration of the war. The U-boats lost the offensive and never regained it.[286] (Note the chart of cumulative attacks on U-boats and shipping in Appendix B.)

Grand Admiral Karl Doenitz described in his memoirs this change in the defenses along the East Coast. He noted that by the end of April his U-boat successes had dropped dramatically. He attributed this to the introduction of convoys, which he considered a turning point in his offensive. For long periods the U-boats could not find shipping to attack.[287] As a result, Doenitz sent his U-boats after easier targets in the Caribbean, but successes there began to decline by the end of June 1942 with the gradual establishment of a convoy system.[288] Doenitz therefore switched his emphasis to the use of U-boats in "wolf packs" to attack mid-Atlantic convoys.

Air power, as a single factor, proved severely disruptive to the wolf packs' tactics. Aircraft kept the U-boats on the defensive, which made it difficult for them to pursue convoys. In every convoy region, air patrols became a constant menace.[289] Doenitz found that in conjunction with the convoys along America's East Coast, air and surface attacks on U-boats continued to increase during the summer of 1942. With the loss of several U-boats during July, he decided to withdraw most of them from America's coast.[290] A few U-boats continued to prowl the area, but their earlier level of activity and success was over.

After the war Doenitz commented that the conclusion could have been dramatically different had he received the men and resources to produce U-boats in the numbers he wanted. He charged that Hitler was fixated on land campaigns and failed to realize the importance of naval warfare even though Germany was at war with two of the world's greatest sea powers. He added that his leaders failed to learn from World War I when they entered a conflict without sufficient U-boats to crush enemy sea traffic. By entering World War II unprepared, they quickly lost the advantage and the offensive.[291]

Near the end of the war, plans were again made to deploy more U-boats against America's East Coast. These plans died along with Adolf Hitler, who killed himself in Berlin on 30 April 1945. Doenitz found that, ironically, he would be the one to call an end to the U-boat campaign, as he was elevated to the position of supreme command in Germany after Hitler's suicide. In a broadcast on 4 May 1945 he instructed all U-boats to cease hostilities and return to their bases. Following the signing of the formal capitulation on 7 May, all of the U-boats at sea were ordered to surrender to any Allied vessel. When the month was over, a total of 49 U-boats had surrendered at sea, while another 211 were scuttled, mostly in the Baltic, to avoid capture. Seven of those that surrendered did so in the western Atlantic to the U.S. Fleet.[292]

The battle of the Atlantic had come to an end. Germany's operation *Paukenschlag* had been silenced with grim finality. Approximately 820 U-boats, including the type VII series, participated in the battle of the Atlantic, of which 781 were destroyed. Furthermore, of the approximately 40,000 German sailors who went to sea in U-boats, 30,000 never returned.[293] With the final defeat of Germany's great U-boat fleet came the end of their threat to the Fifth Naval District. Historians will continue to recognize the courage and outstanding seamanship of those U-boat crews that challenged the Atlantic to attack America's East Coast, but, in the end, the patient development of an ASW program in the Fifth Naval District and its skilled implementation by the Atlantic Fleet played a critical role in deciding the outcome and closing the final chapter on the U-boat story. As a testimony to its success and importance to the final outcome in World War II, the development of ASW continues to be the keystone in America's naval warfare strategy. That is a fitting memorial to those heroic and tenacious American sailors, soldiers, airmen, and civilians who had the perseverance to concentrate their efforts on ASW at the beginning of World War II and final defeat of the "Wolf at the Door."

# APPENDIX A

## *LIST OF ATTACKS BY THE ENEMY IN WATERS OF THE FIFTH NAVAL DISTRICT*

| # | Date | Time | Position | Name | Nationality | Type | Tonnage | How attacked | Result |
|---|------|------|----------|------|-------------|------|---------|--------------|--------|
| 1. | 01-17-42 | 2040 | 35-16 N 74-00 W | SS ALLAN JACKSON | Am. | Tkr. | 6635 | | Sunk |
| 2. | 01-19-42 | 0150 | 35-00 N 72-30 W | SS LADY HAWKINS | Br. Pass. | Cgo. | 7988 | T | Sunk |
| 3. | 01-19-42 | 0215 | 35-24 N 75-21 W | SS CITY OF ATLANTA | Am. | Cgo. | 5269 | T&S | Sunk |
| 4. | 01-19-42 | 0340 | 35-27 N 75-22 W | SS MALAY | Am. | Tkr. | 8207 | T&S | Damaged |
| 5. | 01-19-42 | 0500 | 35-26 N 75-20 W | SS CILTVAIRA | Lat. | Cgo. | 3779 | T | Sunk |

**LEGEND:  T = Torpedo   S = Shelled   M = Mine**

115

| No. | Date | Time | Position | Ship | Nat. | Type | Tons | | Status |
|---|---|---|---|---|---|---|---|---|---|
| 6. | 01-23-42 | 1945 | 34-54 N 75-13 W | MV EMPIRE GEM | Br. | Tkr. | 8139 | T | Sunk |
| 7. | 01-23-42 | 1955 | 34-50 N 75-20 W | SS VENORE | Am. | Ore carr. | 8016 | T | Sunk |
| 8. | 01-27-42 | 0245 | 37-45 N 74-53 W | SS FRANCIS E. POWELL | Am. | Tkr. | 7096 | T | Sunk |
| 9. | 01-30-42 | 1105 | 37-10 N 73-58 W | SS ROCHESTER | Am. | Tkr. | 6836 | T&S | Sunk |
| 10. | 01-31-42 | 2135 | 37-33 N 69-21 W | SS TACOMA STAR | Br. | Cgo. | 7924 | T | Sunk |
| 11. | 02-01-42 | 2020 | 36-00 N 74-00 W | MV AMERIKALAND | Swd. | Ore carr. | 15355 | T | Sunk |
| 12. | 02-08-42 | 0330 | 37-05 N 74-46 W | SS OCEAN VENTURE | Br. | Cgo. | 7174 | T | Sunk |
| 13. | 02-11-42 | 2050 | 35-00 N 72-27 W | SS BLINK | Nor. | Cgo. | 2701 | T | Sunk |

| No. | Date | Time | Position | Ship | Nationality | Cargo | Tons | Type | Result |
|---|---|---|---|---|---|---|---|---|---|
| 14. | 02-15-42 | 0030 | 36-31 N 75-30 W | SS BUARQUE | Brz. | Cgo. | 5152 | T | Sunk |
| 15. | 02-16-42 | 2032 | 36-56 N 75-56 W | SS E.H. BLUM | Am. | Tkr. | 11615 | M ? | Damaged |
| 16. | 02-18-42 | 1245 | 37-30 N 75-00 W | SS OLINDA | Brz. | Cgo. | 6400 | T | Sunk |
| 17. | 02-27-42 | 0030 | 35-36 N 75-16 W | SS MARORE | Am. carr. | Ore | 8215 | T&S | Sunk |
| 18. | 03-07-42 | 1510 | 35-15 N 73-50 W | SS ARABUTAN | Brz. | Cgo. | 7800 | T | Sunk |
| 19. | 03-11-42 | 0200 | 34-37 N 76-17 W | SS CARIBSEA | Am. | Cgo. | 2609 | T | Sunk |
| 20. | 03-13-42 | 1135 | 37-35 N 72-34 W | SS TREPCA | Yug. carr. | Ore | 5042 | T | Sunk |
| 21. | 03-14-42 | 2323 | 34-25 N 76-29 W | SS OLEAN | Am. | Tkr. | 7118 | T | Damaged |

| No. | Date | Time | Coordinates | Ship | Nat. | Type | Tons | T&S | Status |
|---|---|---|---|---|---|---|---|---|---|
| 22. | 03-15-42 | 0122 | 34-21 N 76-37 W | SS ARIO | Am. | Tkr. | 6970 | T&S | Sunk |
| 23. | 03-16-42 | 1400 | 35-07 N 75-22 W | MS AUSTRALIA | Am. | Tkr. | 11628 | T | Sunk |
| 24. | 03-16-42 | 2017 | 36-59 N 74-05 W | MV SAN DEMETRIO | Br. | Tkr. | 8703 | T | Sunk |
| 25. | 03-16-42 | 2045 | 35-50 N 73-58 W | SS CEIBA | Hon. | Cgo. | 1698 | T | Sunk |
| 26. | 03-17-42 | 1750 | 35-05 N 75-21 W | SS ACME | Am. | Tkr. | 6878 | T | Damaged |
| 27. | 03-17-42 | 1915 | 35-05 N 75-23 W | SS KASSANDRA LOULOUDIS | Grk. | Cgo. | 5106 | T | Sunk |
| 28. | 03-18-42 | 0235 | 34-50 N 75-35 W | SS E.M. CLARK | Am. | Tkr. | 9647 | T | Sunk |
| 29. | 03-18-42 | 2210 | 34-22 N 76-48 W | SS W.E. HUTTON | Am. | Tkr. | 7076 | T | Sunk |

| No. | Date | Time | Position | Ship | Nat. | Type | Tonnage | S/T | Fate |
|---|---|---|---|---|---|---|---|---|---|
| 30. | 03-18-42 | 2230 | 34-25 N 76-44 W | SS PAPOOSE | Am. | Tkr. | 5939 | T | Sunk |
| 31. | 03-19-42 | 1015 | 35-06 N 75-23 W | SS LIBERATOR | Am. | Cgo. | 7720 | T | Sunk |
| 32. | 03-19-42 | 2250 | 34-27 N 76-31 W | SS GULF OF MEXICO | Am. | Tkr. | 7807 | S | Escaped |
| 33. | 03-20-42 | 0005 | 34-21 N 76-32 W | MV MERCURY SUN | Am. | Tkr. | 8893 | S | Escaped |
| 34. | 03-20-42 | 1430 | 37-00 N 69-00 W | SS OAKMAR | Am. | Cgo. | 9000 | S | Sunk |
| 35. | 03-26-42 | 0858 | 34-53 N 75-22 W | SS DIXIE ARROW | Am. | Tkr. | 8046 | T | Sunk |
| 36. | 03-26-42 | 1930 | 36-36 N 74-45 W | SS EQUIPOISE | Pan. | Cgo. | 6210 | T | Sunk |
| 37. | 03-29-42 | 1345 | 35-16 N 74-42 W | MV CITY OF NEW YORK | Am. | Cgo. Pass. | 8272 | T | Sunk |

| No. | Date | Time | Position | Name | Nat. | Type | Tonnage | | Status |
|---|---|---|---|---|---|---|---|---|---|
| 38. | 03-31-42 | 0210 | 37-34 N 75-25 W | ALLEGHENY | Am. | Barge | 914 | S | Sunk |
| 39. | 03-31-42 | 0210 | 37-34 N 75-25 W | ONTARIO | Am. | Barge | 490 | S | Damaged |
| 40. | 03-31-42 | 0210 | 37-34 N 75-25 W | BARNEGAT | Am. | Barge | 914 | S | Sunk |
| 41. | 03-31-42 | 0210 | 37-34 N 75-25 W | SS MENOMINEE | Am. | Tug | 441 | S | Sunk |
| 42. | 04-01-42 | 0017 | 36-50 N 75-49 W | SS TIGER | Am. | Tkr. | 5992 | T | Sunk |
| 43. | 04-01-42 | 0920 | 35-16 N 74-32 W | SS RIO BLANCO | Br. | Cgo. | 4086 | T | Sunk |
| 44. | 04-02-42 | 0123 | 34-13 N 76-11 W | SS LIEBRE | Am. | Tkr. | 7057 | S | Damaged |
| 45. | 04-02-42 | 2115 | 37-46 N 75-04 W | SS DAVID H. ATWATER | Am. | Col. | 2438 | S | Sunk |

| | Date | Time | Position | Ship | Nat. | Type | Tons | | Result |
|---|---|---|---|---|---|---|---|---|---|
| —. | 04-02-42 | 2210 | 35-54 N 75-26 W | MV ESSO AUGUSTA | Am. | Tkr. | 11237 | ? | Escaped |
| 46. | 04-03-42 | 0555 | 36-25 N 72-22 W | SS OTHO | Am. | Cgo. Pass. | 4832 | T | Sunk |
| 47. | 04-04-42 | 2140 | 36-08 N 75-32 W | SS BYRON D. BENSON | Am. | Tkr. | 7953 | T | Sunk |
| 48. | 04-06-42 | 0200 | 34-36 N 75-55 W | MV BIDWELL | Am. | Tkr. | 6837 | T | Damaged |
| 49. | 04-06-42 | 2215 | 35-07 N 75-19 W | MV BRITISH SPLENDOUR | Br. | Tkr. | 7138 | T | Sunk |
| 50. | 04-07-42 | 0435 | 35-08 N 75-22 W | SS LANCING | Nor. | Tkr. | 7866 | T | Sunk |
| 51. | 04-09-42 | 0158 | 34-28 N 75-56 W | SS MALCHACE | Am. | Cgo. | 3516 | T | Sunk |
| 52. | 04-09-42 | 0350 | 34-27 N 76-16 W | SS ATLAS | Am. | Tkr. | 7058 | T | Sunk |

| No. | Date | Time | Position | Ship | Nat. | Type | Tons | T/S | Status |
|---|---|---|---|---|---|---|---|---|---|
| 53. | 04-09-42 | 2300 | 35-35 N 75-06 W | MV SAN DELFINO | Br. | Tkr. | 8702 | T | Sunk |
| 54. | 04-10-42 | 0020 | 34-25 N 76-00 W | SS TAMAULIPAS | Am. | Tkr. | 6943 | T | Sunk |
| 55. | 04-11-42 | 0721 | 34-25 N 76-30 W | SS HARRY F. SINCLAIR | Am. | Tkr. | 6151 | T | Damaged |
| 56. | 04-11-42 | 1633 | 34-23 N 75-35 W | SS ULYSSES | Br. | Cgo. Pass. | 14647 | T | Sunk |
| 57. | 04-14-42 | 0920 | 35-08 N 75-18 W | SS EMPIRE THRUSH | Br. | Cgo. | 6160 | T | Sunk |
| 58. | 04-16-42 | 1203 | 35-35 N 72-48 W | SS DESERT LIGHT | Pan. | Cgo. | 2231 | T | Sunk |
| 59. | 04-16-42 | 2150 | 35-34 N 70-08 W | SS ALCOA GUIDE | Am. | Cgo. | 4834 | S | Sunk |
| 60. | 04-18-42 | 1835 | 35-32 N 75-19 W | SS AXTELL J. BYLES | Am. | Tkr. | 8955 | T | Damaged |

| No. | Date | Time | Position | Ship Name | Flag | Type | Tonnage | Prop. | Fate |
|---|---|---|---|---|---|---|---|---|---|
| 61. | 04-20-42 | 1830 | 36-11 N 75-07 W | SS CHENANGO | Pan. | Cgo. | 3106 | T | Sunk |
| 62. | 04-24-42 | 1745 | 36-39 N 70-52 W | SS EMPIRE DRUM | Br. | Frt. | 7340 | T | Sunk |
| 63. | 04-29-42 | 2150 | 34-21 N 76-24 W | SS ASHKHABAD | Rus. | Cgo. | 5284 | T | Sunk |
| 64. | 05-18-42 | 0611 | 34-45 N 75-38 W | SS C.J. BARKDULL | Pan. | Tkr. | 6733 | T | Escaped |
| 65. | 06-01-42 | 0615 | 36-16 N 69-08 W | SS WEST NOTOS | Am. | Cgo. | 5492 | S | Sunk |
| 66. | 06-11-42 | 0640 | 34-52 N 75-45 W | SS F.W. ABRAMS | Am. | Tkr. | 9310 | M ? | Sunk |
| 67. | 06-15-42 | 1705 | 36-51 N 75-51 W | SS ROBERT C. TUTTLE | Am. | Tkr. | 11615 | M | Sunk |
| 68. | 06-15-42 | 1733 | 36-51 N 75-51 W | MV ESSO AUGUSTA | Am. | Tkr. | 11237 | M | Damaged |

| No. | Date | Time | Ship Name | Position | Nat. | Type | Tons | Prop. | Status |
|---|---|---|---|---|---|---|---|---|---|
| 69. | 06-15-42 | 1915 | HMS KINGSTON CEYLONITE | 36-50 N 75-55 W | Br. | Trawl. | 500 | M | Sunk |
| 70. | 06-17-42 | 0745 | SS SANTORE | 36-52 N 75-49 W | Am. | Ore Carr. | 7117 | M | Sunk |
| 71. | 06-19-42 | 0220 | USS YP-389 | 34-53 N 75-31 W | Am. | Armed Trawl. | 165 | S | Sunk |
| 72. | 06-24-42 | 0330 | SS LJUBICA MATKOVIC | 34-30 N 75-40 W | Yug. | Cgo. | 3289 | T | Sunk |
| 73. | 06-24-42 | 1923 | SS NORDAL | 34-30 N 75-40 W | Pan. | Cgo. | 3845 | T | Sunk |
| 74. | 06-24-42 | 1927 | SS MANUELA | 34-30 N 75-40 W | Am. | Cgo. | 4749 | T | Sunk |
| 75. | 06-25-42 | 2010 | MV TAMESIS | 34-59 N 75-41 W | Nor. | Cgo. Pass. | 7256 | M | Damaged |
| 76. | 06-27-42 | 1615 | MV MOLDANGER | 36-50 N 69-22 W | Nor. | Cgo. | 6827 | T | Sunk |

| No. | Date | Time | Position | Ship | Nat. | Type | Tonnage | | Status |
|---|---|---|---|---|---|---|---|---|---|
| 77. | 06-27-42 | 1107 | 34-45 N 75-22 W | MV BRITISH FREEDOM | Br. | Tkr. | 6985 | T | Damaged |
| 78. | 06-28-42 | 1216 | 35-01 N 75-05 W | SS WM. ROCKEFELLER | Am. | Tkr. | 14054 | T | Sunk |
| 79. | 06-30-42 | 1925 | 35-04 N 70-46 W | SS CITY OF BIRMINGHAM | Am. | Cgo. | 5861 | T | Sunk |
| 80. | 07-15-42 | 1620 | 34-51 N 75-22 W | SS CHILORE | Am. | Cgo. | 8310 | T&M | Sunk |
| 81. | 07-15-42 | 1621 | 34-51 N 75-22 W | MV J.A. MOWINCKEL | Pan. | Tkr. | 11148 | T&M | Damaged |
| 82. | 07-15-42 | 1622 | 34-51 N 75-22 W | MV BLUEFIELDS | Nic. | Cgo. | 2063 | T | Sunk |
| 83. | 05-04-43 | 0825 | 34-10 N 76-05 W | SS PANAM | Pan. | Cgo. | 7277 | T | Sunk |
| 84. | 08-05-43 | 1542 | 37-22 N 74-25 W | SS PLYMOUTH | Am. | Cgo. | 2265 | T&M | Sunk |

| | | | | | | | | | |
|---|---|---|---|---|---|---|---|---|---|
| 85. | 12-04-43 | 0400 | 34-30 N 74-32 W | SS LIBERTAD | Cuban | Cgo. | 5441 | T | Sunk |
| 86. | 09-12-44 | 0030 | 33-30 N 75-40 W | SS GEORGE ADE | Am. | Cgo. | 7176 | T | Damaged |

## APPENDIX B

### *HERBERT WERNER'S U-230 MINING NARRATIVE*

"When the sun began to rise, we dived to maintain secrecy. Traveling westward slowly at a depth of 40 meters, we came within 30 miles of Cape Charles. Because we knew nothing of the U.S. defenses, we manned action stations and kept the aft tube ready to shoot in case of a surprise attack. Shortly after noon, the soundman reported increasing propeller noise. The chief raised the boat to periscope depth for the Captain (Captain Paul Siegmann) to investigate. To Siegmann's surprise, we were dead ahead of a small convoy—much closer than the gear indicated. There were four destroyers shepherding only seven cargo ships. Suddenly the Captain cried, 'Boat is coming up, hold her down, bridge is breaking surface, down with her, Chief!'

"Friederich (*U-230*'s helmsman) applied all emergency measures—no reaction. 'What the hell is wrong with this sloop, dive, dive fast!' hollered Siegmann.

"...Then, slowly the boat drilled herself into a layer of heavy-density water. Just as her stern moved into the specifically heavier stratum of water, a spread of six charges detonated in closest proximity. The explosions propelled the boat below the thermal shift, and her screws, turning in maximum revolutions, drove her downward until she touched the sandy bottom. The ASDIC pings released by the U.S. destroyers chirped through the shallow water, but did not hit our hull with the usual force; the sound waves were largely refracted by the dense layer of heavy water above us. For almost two hours the hunters nervously screened the depths, vainly seeking something to attack. Then they departed without spending one more depth charge on us.

"We surfaced at nightfall. *U-230* pushed swiftly and relentlessly ahead. Three hours passed in apprehension and mounting excitement. Then, port ahead, a vague glow crept over the horizon—the lights of Norfolk. Minutes later, Borchert (*U-230* watchstander) shouted, 'America dead ahead!'

"We had reached our destination. Time: 2325. Date: July 27, 1943.

"As the thin line of the coast emerged from the water, Prager's voice drifted up from the darkness of the control room: 'Boat is four miles east of Cape Charles. Suggest changing course to two-three-five.'

"'Very well,' acknowledged Siegmann, 'Exec, have the eggs ready for the drop.'

"I ordered the four front tubes flooded and the doors opened. *U-230* proceeded at high speed, leaving Fisherman's Island on starboard. Our depth finder sounded out the water. Prager took constant bearings. Our presence was still a secret.

"When we reached the halfway mark between Cape Charles in the north and Cape Henry in the south, Siegmann turned the bow of his boat into the shallow waters of the Chesapeake Bay. Surprisingly, not a single enemy vessel was there to stop us as the lights of Norfolk became clearly visible on port (here Werner may have mistaken the distant lights of Virginia Beach for Little Creek or Norfolk, Virginia). The American sailors must have been at a big party that night; they were surely not at sea. As we passed the Naval Base, the silhouette of the illuminated city rose sharply against the dark sky. Land rose all around us as we penetrated deeper into the Bay.

"Two hours after midnight, we detected several cargo ships heading for the open sea. Their sudden appearance wrecked our plan to drop the mines that night. We had no time to dive and no alternative but to retreat into darkness. For one long minute, our broadside was exposed unseen as *U-230* made a full turn. Then we sped ahead of the vessels out of the Bay. We saw one of them turn north and three veer south before they all dissolved in the night. We continued dashing eastward, covering 30 miles in two hours, then laid *U-230* aground in shallow water and waited for the next evening to arrive.

"July 28. At 2145, when the last rays of the sun were extinguished, we surfaced and raced with highest revolutions back into Chesapeake Bay. Again we passed the line Cape Charles—Cape Henry. To the left lay Norfolk, and the American Navy was again celebrating in port. The Bay was deserted; only *U-230* made the sounds that disturbed the serenity of the night. It was near midnight when Borchert spotted a shadow suddenly mounting in the blackness dead ahead. We slowed down immediately. But the shadow grew so fast into a giant that Siegmann had to stop both engines to prevent our crashing into the stern of a merchant ship. Obviously, she was heading toward Baltimore. She sailed at a mere eight knots, rather slow for our timetable. But since we could not tell her skipper to hurry, we had to adjust our speed and follow in her wake. For several minutes we used our powerful binoculars to survey the American countryside.

At 0210, Siegmann reckoned we had proceeded far enough into the Bay. Swinging his boat on opposite course, he headed back toward the flickering lights of Norfolk. As *U-230* steadied on her course, I lowered myself into the darkened hull to activate and release the mines. Five minutes later, the first egg dropped from its tube with a soft splash. Three minutes later, egg number two followed, then number three—and the first tube was empty.

As the mines were discharged in regular intervals the tubes were speedily reloaded. Fresh mines were lifted from their racks by trolleys and chains and cautiously moved into place. The hot bow room steamed with the sweat of half-naked bodies and resounded with the clanking of chains. The drop went smoothly and lasted one hour and 50 minutes. After it was all over, I hurried to the bridge and reported, 'Twenty-four eggs dropped into Uncle Sam's front yard.'

"Replied Siegmann, 'Both engines full ahead, steer course nine-oh.' The boat gained momentum fast and scurried along at 17 knots, past Norfolk, past Fisherman's Island, toward a new morning sky. We dived around 0600 without any interference and floated into the open sea far below surface."

Thus ends Herbert Werner's fantastic, and many argue, unbelievable, story on mining the shipping channel within the lights of Norfolk.

## APPENDIX C

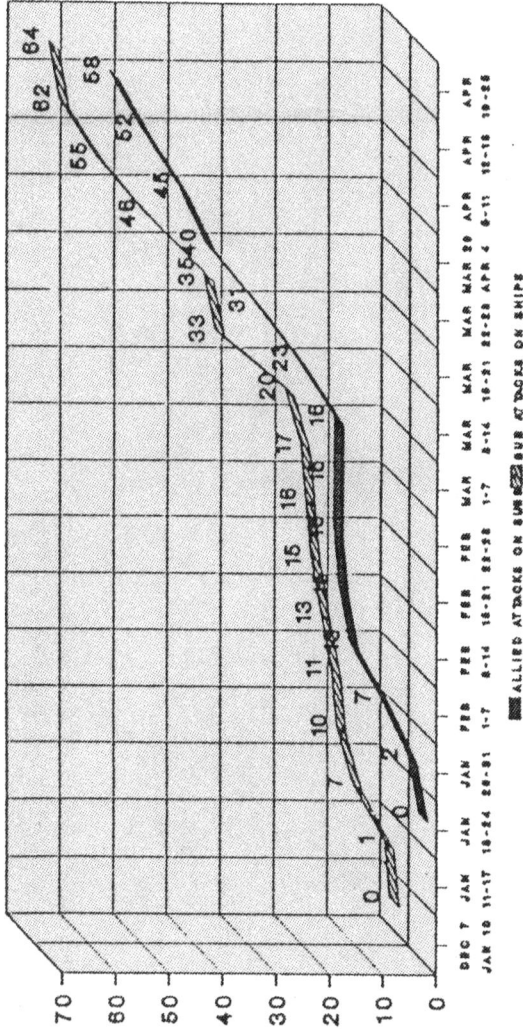

SUBMARINE ACTIVITY
FIFTH NAVAL DISTRICT
CHART 1 (CUMULATIVE)

DEC 7, 1941 – APR 25, 1942
A–MARCH 27–START OF DISTRICT CONVOYS
B–APRIL 1–ORGANIZATION OF "KILLER TEAMS"

# SUBMARINE ACTIVITY

## FIFTH NAVAL DISTRICT

### CHART 2 (CUMULATIVE)

APR 7, 1942 - AUG 22, 1942

A—MAY 14—START OF ESF COASTAL CONVOYS

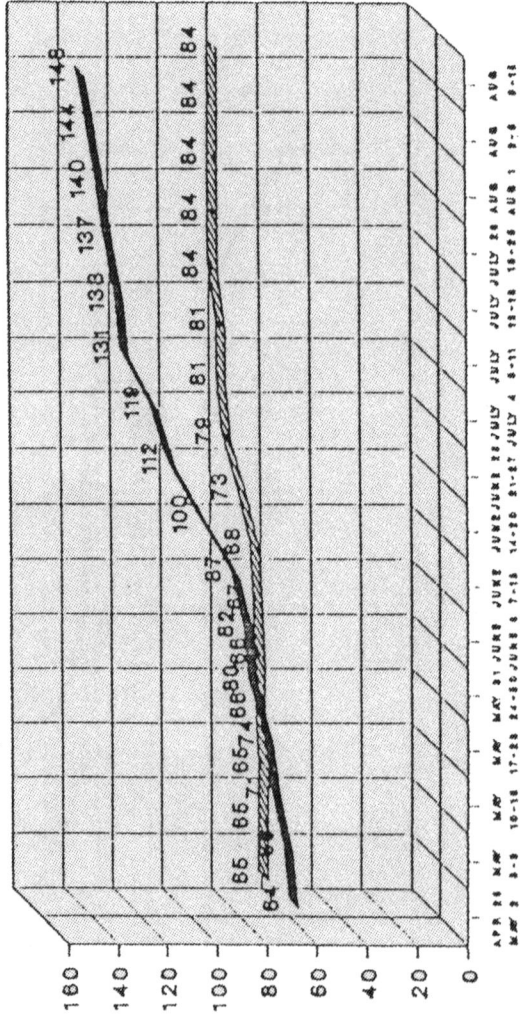

ALLIED ATTACKS ON SUB    SUB ATTACKS ON SHIPS

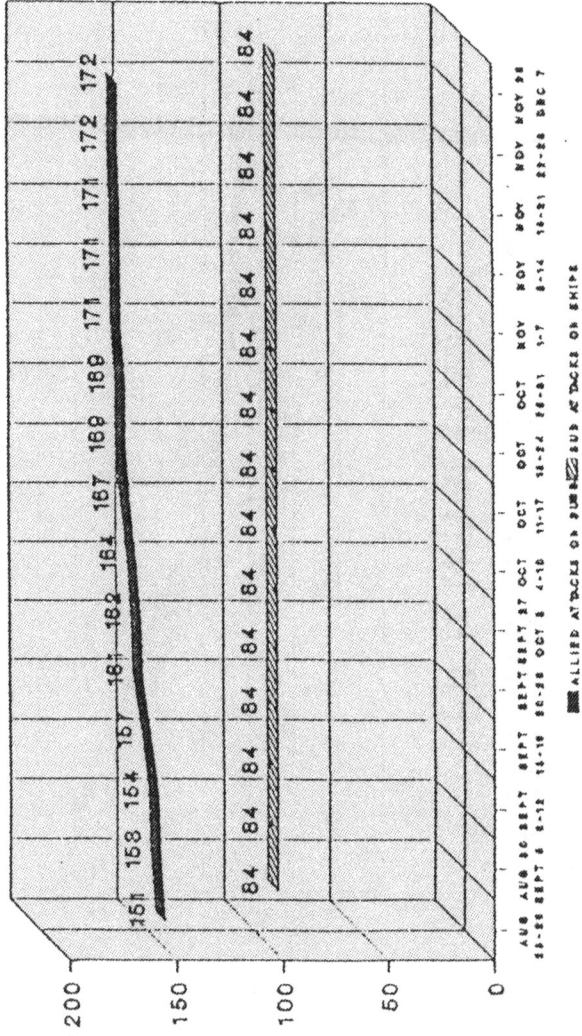

SUBMARINE ACTIVITY
FIFTH NAVAL DISTRICT
CHART 3 (CUMULATIVE)

AUG 23, 1942 – DEC 7, 1942

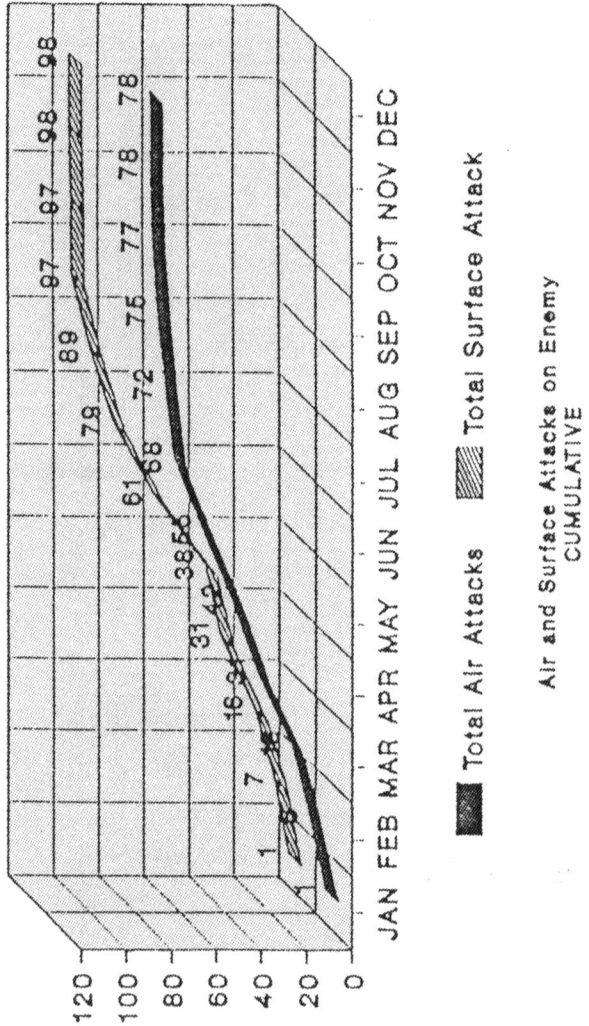

Air and Surface
Attacks on the Enemy
Fifth Naval District

JAN FEB MAR APR MAY JUN JUL AUG SEP OCT NOV DEC

■ Total Air Attacks    ▨ Total Surface Attack

Air and Surface Attacks on Enemy
CUMULATIVE

## ENDNOTES

[1]Arthur A. Ageton, The Naval Officer's Guide (New York: McGraw-Hill, 1943), 65.

[2]Fifth Naval District, "War Diary of Operational Intelligence," n.d., Box no. 390, pp. 1-6, Operational Archives, Naval Historical Center, Washington, D.C.

[3]David Westwood, Anatomy of the Ship — The Type VII U-boat (Annapolis: Naval Institute Press, 1984), 9-12.

[4]Dr. Scott C. Truver, ed., United States Naval Institute Professional Seminar, "ASW: The Navy's Top Warfighting Priority?" USNI, 27 February 1990, pp. 3-4, photocopied.

[5]Fifth Naval District, "War Record of the Fifth Naval District, 1942," 1943, Guide no. 129, p. 1, Operational Archives, Naval Historical Center, Washington, D.C.

[6]Ibid., 2.

[7]Commandant, Fifth Naval District, "History of the Fifth Naval District, 1939-1945," vol. 2, 1946, Guide No. 112, pp. 491-92, Navy Library, Naval Historical Center, Washington, D.C.

[8]Ibid., 677.

[9]Ibid., 678.

[10]Ibid., 679.

[11]Frederick G. Swink, U.S. Coast Guard officer, interview by authors, Tape recording, Norfolk, Virginia, 8 August 1991.

[12]Ibid.

[13]Ibid.

[14]Chief of Naval Operations, "Antisubmarine Warfare in World War II: OEG Report No. 51," (Charles M. Sternhill and Alan M. Thorndike), 1946, Guide No. 435, pp. 25, Operational Archives, Naval Historical Center, Washington, D.C.

[15]Linwood Hudgins, U.S. Coast Guard buoy tender, interview by authors, Tape recording, Portsmouth, Virginia, 11 January 1991.

[16]Ibid.

[17]Ibid.

[18]ibid.

[19]Ibid.

[20]Ibid.

[21]Ibid.

[22]Ibid.

[23]Ibid.

[24]Reinhard Hardegan, captain of U-123, interview by authors, Tape recording, Bremen, Germany, 28 November 1991.

[25]Ibid.

[26]Ibid.

[27]Ibid.

[28]Horst Degen, captain of U-701, interview by authors, Tape recording, Luneburg, Germany, 27 November 1991.

[29]Ibid.

[30]Ibid.

[31]Helmut Rathke, captain of U-352, interview by authors, Tape recording, Flensburg, Germany, 29 November 1991.

[32]Frank Blackford, "When War Was At Our Doorstep," *The Virginian-Pilot and The Ledger-Star*, 17 October 1971.

[33]T.J. Belie, "Roll of Drums," *USNI Proceedings*, United States Naval Institute, April 1983, p. 60.

[34]Ed Offley, "Chesapeake Bay Mined — War Came Close to Home," *The Virginian-Pilot and The Ledger-Star*, 8 July 1982.

[35]Hardegen, interview by authors.

[36]Ibid.

[37]Ibid.

[38]Ibid.

[39]Ibid.

[40]Ibid.

[41]Ibid.

[42]Ibid.

[43]Navy Department, Office of Naval Operations, "Report on the Interrogation of Survivors of U-701 Sunk by U.S. Army Attack Bomber No. 9-29-322, Unit 296 B.S. on July 7, 1942," n.d., Operational Archives, Naval Historical Center, Washington, D.C.

[44]Horst Degan, captain of U-352, interview by authors, Tape recording, Bremen, Germany, 27 November 1991.

[45]Ibid.

[46]Horst Degen, personal memoir "U-701, a German Submarine, Glory and Tragedy 1942," Luneburg, Germany, 14 November 1965. Copy in possession of the authors.

[47]Ibid.

[48]Ibid.

[49]Offley, "Chesapeake Bay Mined."

[50]Degen, personal memoir.

[51]Ibid.

[52]Ibid.

[53]Ibid.

[54]Ibid.

[55]Ibid.

[56]Ibid.

[57]Ibid.

[58]Ibid.

[59]Ibid.

[60]Ibid.

[61]Fifth Naval District, "War Record," 263; Navy Department, Office of the Chief of Naval Operations, "Summary of Statement of Survivors of the SS *Robert C. Tuttle*," n.d., Operational Archives, Naval Historical Center, Washington, D.C.

[62]Fifth Naval District, "War Record," 264; Navy Department, "Summary of Statements by Survivors of the MV *Esso Augusta*," n.d., Operational Archives, Naval Historical Center, Washington, D.C.

[63]Fifth Naval District, "War Record," 265-66; Navy Department, "Summary of Statements by Survivors of HMS *Kingston Ceylonite*." n.d., Operational Archives, Naval Historical Center, Washington, D.C.

[64]Commandant, "History," 602-3.

[65]Ibid., 273-76.

[66]Ibid., 603.

[67]Ibid., 607.

[68]Samuel Eliot Morison, *History of U.S. Naval Operations in World War II*, vol. 10, *The Battle of the Atlantic Won, May 1943 - May 1945* (Boston: Little, Brown, and Company, 1956), 417.

[69]Commandant, Fifth Naval District, "History of the Fifth Naval District, 1939-1945," vol. 2, 1946, Guide No. 112, p. 523, Navy Library, Naval Historical Center, Washington, D.C.

[70]Ibid., 492-93.

[71]Ibid., 494.

[72]Harry Sanders, "King of the Oceans," USNI *Proceedings*, U.S. Naval Institute, August 1974, pp. 52-59.

[73]Commandant, "History," 489.

[74]Ibid., 497.

[75]Ibid., 497.

[76]Ibid., 646.

[77]Ibid., 696.

[78]Ibid., 618.

[79]Ibid., 622-23.

[80]Ibid., 625.

[81]Ibid., 632-33.

[82]Ibid., 583-84.

[83]Ibid., 589-98.

[84]Linwood Hudgins, U.S. Coast Guard buoy tender, Interview by authors, Tape recording, Portsmouth, Virginia, 11 January 1992.

[85]Ibid.

[86]Ibid., 518-20.

[87]Ibid., 521-22.

[88]Rollin L. Tilton, "History of Chesapeake Bay Sector," Fort Monroe, Virginia, 1 March 1945, p. 24, Copy in possession of Lieutenant Colonel Fielding L. Tyler, U.S. Army retired, Virginia Beach, Virginia.

[89]Commandant, "History," 721, 724-25.

[90]Chief of Naval Operations, "Antisubmarine Warfare in World War II: OEG Report No. 25," (Charles M. Sternhill and Alan M. Thorndike), 1946, Guide No. 435, p. 25, Operational Archives, Naval Historical Center, Washington, D.C.

[91]Commandant, "History," 692-93.

[92]Frederick G. Swink, U.S. Coast Guard pickett officer, interview by authors, Tape recording, Norfolk, Virginia, 8 August 1991.

[93]Alan B. Flanders and Captain Arthur C. Johnson, Jr., Guardians of the Capes: History of Pilots and Piloting in Virginia Waters from 1611 to the Present (Lively, Virginia: Brandylane Publishers, 1991), 73.

[94]Ibid.

[95]Ibid.

[96]Ibid.

[97]Ibid.

[98]Ibid., 74.

[99]Fifth Naval District, "War Record of the Fifth Naval District, 1942," 1943, Guide No. 129, p. 461, Operational Archives, Naval Historical Center, Washington, D.C.

[100]Hudgins, interview.

[101]Chief of Naval Operations, "OEG Report," 28-29.

[102]Samuel Eliot Morison, History of U.S. Naval Operations in World War II, vol. 10, The Battle of the Atlantic Won, May 1943 — May 1945 (Boston: Little, Brown, and Company, 1956), 361.

[103]Commandant, "History," 669.

[104]Ibid., 671.

[105]Ibid., 662-63.

[106]Ibid., 666.

[107]Joseph A. Kelly, U.S. Coast Guard pickett officer, interview by authors, Tape recording, Norfolk, Virginia, 13 October 1991.

[108]Ibid.

[109]Ibid.

[110]Ibid.

[111]Ibid.

[112]Ibid.

[113]Ibid.

[114]Ibid.

[115]Ibid.

[116]Ibid.

[117]Ibid.

[118]Ibid.

[119]Ibid.

[120]Ibid.

[121]Ibid.

[122]Ibid.

[123]Ibid.

[124]Ibid.

[125]Ibid.

[126]Ibid.

[127]Ibid.

[128]Ibid., 667-68.

[129]Samuel Eliot Morison, <u>History of U.S. Naval Operations in World War II</u>, vol. 1, <u>The Battle of the Atlantic, September 1939 — May 1943</u> (Boston: Little, Brown, and Company, 1947), 282-83.

[130]World War II Command File, *Atik,* n.d., Operational Archives, Naval Historical Center, Washington, D.C.

[131]Ibid.

[132]Ibid.

[133]Commander in Chief, U.S. Atlantic Fleet, "Commander Fleet Operational Training Command," 1946, Guide No. 143, pp. 285, 290, 296, Navy Library, Naval Historical Center, Washington, D.C.

[134]Harry Clark, Navy ASW instructor, interview by authors, Tape recording, Chesapeake, Virginia, 14 October 1989.

[135]Ibid.

[136]Harry Clark, Interview with author, Chesapeake, Virginia, 14 October 1989.

[137]Commandant, "History," 510-11.

[138]Commander in Chief, "Training Command," 256.

[139]Ibid., 257-58.
[140]Commander in Chief, U.S. Atlantic Fleet, "Commander Fleet Operational Training Command," Guide No. 143, Vol. 8, Chapter 26, pp. 16-17, Operational Archives, Naval Historical Center, Washington, D.C.
[141]Commander in Chief, "Training Command," 256-66, 277.
[142]Commander in Chief, "Commander Fleet Operational Training Command," Chapter 26, pp. 20-21, 26.
[143]Ibid., 20-21.
[144]Ibid., 23-24.
[145]Ibid., 27.
[146]Ibid., 28.
[147]Ibid., 31.
[148]Commandant, Fifth Naval District, "History of the Fifth Naval District, 1939-1945," vol. 2, 1946, Guide No. 112, pp. 697-98, Navy Library, Naval Historical Center, Washington, D.C.
[149]Alpheus J. Chewning, "Buried on Foreign Soil," Virginia Cavalcade, Autumn 1989, pp. 84-95.
[150]Fifth Naval District, "War Record of the Fifth Naval District, 1942," 1943, Guide No. 129, pp. 355-61, Operational Archives, Naval Historical Center, Washington, D.C.
[151]Fifth Naval District, "Sinking of German Submarine U-85, Report on the Disposition of Bodies and Effects," n.d., copy of report in possession of Frank Shield, Virginia Beach, Virginia.
[152]Stanley H. Powell, M.D. Interview with the author, Portsmouth Virginia, 15 May 1990.
[153]Fifth Naval District Intelligence Office, "Sinking of U-85."
[154]Rollin L. Tilton, "History of Chesapeake Bay Sector," Fort Monroe, Virginia, 1 March 1945, p. 33, Copy in possession of Lieutenant Colonel Fielding L. Tyler, U.S. Army retired, Virginia Beach, Virginia.
[155]Commander in Chief, U.S. Atlantic Fleet, Office of Naval Intelligence, "Information on German U-boats No. 1," 1942, Report in possession of Frank Shield, Virginia Beach, Virginia; Tilton, 39.
[156]Hellmut Rathke, captain of U-352, interview by authors, Tape recording, Flensburg, Germany, 29 November 1991.
[157]Ibid.
[158]Ibid.
[159]Horst Degen, captain of U-701, interview by authors, Tape recording, Luneburg, Germany, 27 November 1991.
[160]Ibid.
[161]Harry Kane, U-701: A Real Life "Das Boot," n.d., Virginia Beach Life

Saving Museum, Virginia Beach, Virginia, Videocassette.

[162]Degen interview.

[163]Ibid.

[164]Ibid.

[165]Ibid.

[166]Ibid.

[167]Ibid.

[168]Ibid.

[169]Ibid.

[170]Ibid.

[171]Ibid.

[172]Ibid.

[173]Ibid.

[174]Ibid.

[175]Ibid.

[176]Ibid.

[177]Ibid.

[178]Ibid.

[179]Ibid.

[180]Ibid.

[190]Ibid.

[191]Ibid.

[192]Ibid.

[193]Ibid.

[194]Ibid.

[195]Ibid.

[196]Ibid.

[197]Ibid.

[198]Ibid.

[199]Ibid.

[200]Ibid.; Commandant, "History," 425-32.

[201]Ed Offley, "Confrontation in the Atlantic — The Death of the U-701," The Virginian-Pilot and The Ledger-Star, 9 July 1982.

[202]Fifth Naval District, "War Record," 539-41.

[203]Rollin L. Tilton, "History of Chesapeake Bay Sector," Fort Monroe, Virginia, 1 March 1945, p. 13, Copy in possession of Lieutenant Colonel Fielding L. Tyler, U.S. Army retired, Virginia Beach, Virginia.

[204]Commandant, Fifth Naval District, "History of the Fifth Naval District, 1939-1945," vol. 2, 1946, Guide No. 112, p. 527, Navy Library, Naval Historical Center, Washington, D.C.

[205]Ibid., 525.

[206]Ibid., 536-37.

[207]Ibid., 59.

[208]Ibid., 61.

[209]Commandant, "History," 534.

[210]Tilton, 61.

[211]Ibid., 62.

[212]Fifth Naval District, "War Diary of Operational Intelligence," n.d., Box no. 390, pp. 9-13, Operational Archives, Naval Historical Center, Washington, D.C.

[213]Robert Hasler, Navy intelligence officer, interview by authors, Tape recording, Norfolk, Virginia, 5 November 1992.

[214]Ibid.

[215]Ibid.

[216]Ibid.

[217]Ibid.

[218]Ibid.

[219]Ibid.

[220]Ibid.

[221]Ibid.

[222]Ibid.

[223]Ibid.

[224]Ibid.

[225]Ibid.

[226]Ibid.

[227]Hellmut Rathke, captain of U-352, interview by authors, Tape recording, Flensburg, Germany, 29 November 1991.

[228]Ibid.

[229]Ibid.

[230]Ibid.

[231]Ibid.

[232]Ibid.

[233]Ibid.

[234]Ibid.

[235]Fifth Naval District, "Operational Intelligence," 9-13.

[236]Ibid.

[237]Ibid.

[238]Fifth Naval District, "War Record of the Fifth Naval District, 1942," 1943, Guide No. 129, pp. 51-54, Operational Archives, Naval Historical Center, Washington, D.C.

[239]Fifth Naval District, "Operational Intelligence," 21-22.

[240]Ibid., 22-24.

[241]Ibid., 25-30.

[242]Ibid.

[243]Ibid., 47-50.

[244]Ibid.

[245]Ibid., 51-52.

[246]Ibid., 36-39.

[247]Ibid., 19-20.

[248]Ibid., 24.

[249]Ibid., 45-47.

[250]Rollin L. Tilton, "History of Chesapeake Bay Sector," Fort Monroe, Virginia, 1 March 1945, pp. 66, 72, Copy in possession of Lieutenant Colonel Fielding L. Tyler, U.S. Army retired, Virginia Beach, Virginia.

[251]Fifth Naval District, "Operational Intelligence," 14-17.

[252]Rollin L. Tilton, "History of Chesapeake Bay Sector," Fort Monroe, Virginia, 1 March 1945, p. 4, Copy in possession of Lieutenant Colonel Fielding L. Tyler, U.S. Army retired, Virginia Beach, Virginia.

[253]Commandant, Fifth Naval District, "History of the Fifth Naval District, 1939-1945," vol. 2, 1946, Guide No. 112, p. 619, Navy Library, Naval Historical Center, Washington, D.C.

[254]Tilton, 1, 4-6.

[255]Richard P. Weinert, and Colonel Robert Arthur, *Defenders of the Chesapeake - The Story of Fort Monroe* (Annapolis: Leeward Publications, 1978), 242.

[256]Lieutenant Colonel Fielding L. Tyler, "Fort Story, Virginia, World War II Armament Tour," n.d., Life-Saving Museum of Virginia, Virginia Beach, Virginia.

[257]Weinert and Arthur, 220.

[258]Tyler.

[259]Ibid.

[260]Ibid.

[261]Tilton, 45.

[262]Commandant, "History," 619.

[263]Tilton, 12.

[264]Ibid., 21.

[265]Samuel Eliot Morison, <u>History of U.S. Naval Operations in World War II</u>, vol. 1, <u>The Battle of the Atlantic, September 1939 — May 1943</u> (Boston: Little, Brown, and Company, 1947), 240-41.

[266]Ibid., 242-46.

[267]Chief of Naval Operations, "Antisubmarine Warfare in World War II: OEG Report No. 51," (Charles M. Sternhill and Alan M. Thorndike), 1946, Guide No. 435, p. 29, Operational Archives, Naval Historical Center, Washington, D.C.

[268]Basil Collier, The Airship-A History, (New York: G.P. Putnam and Sons, 1974), 246.

[269]John A. Fahey, airship captain, interview by authors, Tape recording, Norfolk, Virginia, 4 November 1992.

[270]Ibid.

[271]Ibid.

[272]Ibid.

[273]Ibid.

[274]Ibid.

[275]Ibid.

[276]Ibid.

[277]Ibid.

[278]Ibid.

[279]Ibid.

[280]Ibid.

[281]Ibid.

[282]Fifth Naval District, "War Diary of Operational Intelligence," n.d., Box no. 390, p. 360, Operational Archives, Naval Historical Center, Washington, D.C.

[283]Commander in Chief, U.S. Atlantic Fleet, "Air Force Atlantic Fleet History," vol. 7, 1946, Guide No. 142, p. 12, Navy Library, Naval Historical Center, Washington, D.C.

[284]Fifth Naval District, "War Diary," 539-41; Fifth Naval District, "War Diary-Eastern Sea Frontier Chesapeake Group," n.d., Operational Archives, Naval Historical Center, Washington, D.C.

[285]Ibid.

[286]Commandant, Fifth Naval District, "History of the Fifth Naval District, 1939-1945," vol. 2, 1946, Guide No. 112, pp. 699-700, Navy Library, Naval Historical Center, Washington, D.C.

[287]Fifth Naval District, "War Record of the Fifth Naval District, 1942," 1943, Guide No. 129, p. 461, Operational Archives, Naval Historical Center, Washington, D.C.

[288]U.S. Naval Administration in World War II, "BUORD Underwater Ordnance," vol. 9, 1940, Guide No. 78, pp. 252-55, Navy Library, Naval Historical Center, Washington, D.C.

[289]Morison, History 1:211.

[290]U.S. Naval Administration, "BUORD," 256.

[291]Morison, History 1:212.

[292]Ibid., 213, 225-26.

[293]Commandant, "History," 746.

[294]Fifth Naval District, "War Record of the Fifth Naval District, 1942," 1943, Guide No. 129, p. 8, Operational Archives, Naval Historical Center, Washington, D.C.

[295]Ibid.

[296]Karl Doenitz, Memoirs: Ten Years and Twenty Days (Annapolis: Naval Institute Press, 1990), 220.

[297]Ibid., 221-22.

[298]Ibid., 242.

[299]Ibid., 250.

[300]Ibid., 333.

[301]Commander in Chief, U.S. Atlantic Fleet, vol. 1 (bound in 2 vols.), 1946, Guide No. 138, pp. 766-67, Navy Library, Naval Historical Center, Washington, D.C.

[302]Peter Cremer, U-boat Commander (Annapolis: Naval Institute Press, 1984), xi.

# BIBLIOGRAPHY

## Primary Sources

### U.S. Navy Official Publications

All sources, in this section only, originated from either the Operational Archives or the Library located at the Naval Historical Center (N.H.C.) in Washington, D.C. Each source indicates the area of the N.H.C. from which it came.

Andrew, Akidmore, and Madigan Hyland. "Survey of Congested War Production Areas for the Army and Navy Munitions Board." Joint Army and Navy Munitions Board. 15 January 1943. Guide No. 217. Operational Archives.Declassified. Detailed survey of the many features of the cities of Tidewater pertinent to the war effort of World War II. Specific data given for population, manpower, housing, health care, school, recreation, water supply, fire departments, police departments, markets, food supply, fuel, power, communications, and transportation. [N.H.C.]

Chief of Naval Operations. (Sternhill, Charles M., and Alan M. Thorndike.) "Antisubmarine Warfare in World War II: OEG Report No. 51." Chief of Naval Operations, 1946. Guide No. 435. Operational Archives. Declassified. General, overall report on antisubmarine warfare throughout World War II. Good details on the use of convoys, aircraft, and patrol vessels. Information on technological innovations included. [N.H.C.]

Commandant. Fifth Naval District. "History of the Fifth Naval District, 1939-1945." Vol. 2, 1946. Guide No. 112. Navy Library. Declassified. Separate sections describe elements of defenses within the Fifth Naval District. Covers Navy underwater defenses of the Chesapeake Bay, efforts to keep the channels free of mines, patrols of the endangered areas, efforts directed at protecting shipping, and security measures for the harbors. [N.H.C.]

Commander in Chief, U.S. Atlantic Fleet. "Air Force Atlantic Fleet History." Vol. 7, 1946. Guide No. 142. Navy Library. Declassified. Report describes the increasing role of aviation in antisubmarine warfare. Describes the air force and the Atlantic Fleet, including its origins and mission, as well as highlights from its operations. [N.H.C.]

_____. "An Administrative History of Destroyers, Atlantic Fleet." Vol. 6, 1946. Guide No. 141. Navy Library. Declassified. This report describes the function and strategies behind the participation of destroyers in a "killer group." Overview of the battle of the Atlantic provided also. [N.H.C.]

_____. "Commander in Chief. U.S. Atlantic Fleet." Vol. 1 (bound in 2 vols.), 1946. Guide No. 138. Navy Library. Declassified. Details on the last days of the German U-boat offensive. Illustrates how Grand Admiral Karl Doenitz assumed the position of supreme command in Germany following the suicide of Adolf Hitler. Describes the orders he issued bringing the hostilities to an end. [N.H.C.]

_____. "Commander Fleet Operational Training Command." Vol. 8, 1946. Guide No. 143. Navy Library. Declassified. Chapter 26 has details on the development and operation of the Antisubmarine Unit in Norfolk, Virginia. Information on training included. Chapter 28 describes the Fleet Sonar School in Key West, Florida. Chapter 15 describes the Minecraft Training Center. [N.H.C.]

_____. "Convoy and Routing." 1945. Guide No. 11. Navy Library. Declassified. Report describes the administration and organization of convoys along the East Coast during World War II. Details on the system's beginning include a chronological list of the first convoys. Other details include how convoys' movements, schedules, routes, speed, and voyage times were controlled. [N.H.C.]

Fifth Naval District. "War Diary — Eastern Sea Frontier Chesapeake Group." N.d. Operational Archives. Declassified. Day-by-day report on enemy activity in the Fifth Naval District. [N.H.C.]

_____. "War Diary of Operational Intelligence." n.d. Box No. 390. Operational Archives. Declassified. Detailed report on Naval Intelligence operations during World War II. Data on coastal information, antisubmarine warfare and operations intelligence. Appendix B lists enemy attacks in Fifth Naval District waters. [N.H.C.]

_____. "War Record of the Fifth Naval District, 1942." Naval Districts, 1943. Guide No. 129. Operational Archives. Declassified. Contains excellent graphs, charts, maps, and photographs. Descriptions of all Navy-recorded activities of both enemy and American vessels in the Fifth Naval District. Description of each ship sunk, both domestic and foreign. Text describes an attack on a U-boat by the Navy's non-rigid airship K-7. Appendix C describes the Navy's "Killer Team" techniques for hunting U-boats. Appendix D describes how convoys were used. Also has listing of all attacks conducted by the United States Navy in Fifth Naval District waters, plus contains list of all ships sunk. [N.H.C.]

Navy Department. Office of the Chief of Naval Operations. "Mine Warfare in the Naval Establishment." n.d. Guide No. 15. Navy Library. Declassified. Comprehensive Naval report on the use of minefields to protect harbors and ports in the Fifth Naval District. Administrative and operational procedures given. Several accidents covered also. No maps or charts, though. Numerous typing errors in text. [N.H.C.]

_____. "Summary of Statements by Survivors of the MV *Esso Augusta*. n.d. Operational Archives. Declassified. Gives exact location, time, and circumstances surrounding the sinking of the oil tanker MV *Esso Augusta*. Ship specifications are also given. [N.H.C.]

_____. "Summary of Statements by Survivors of the HMS *Kingston Ceylonite*." n.d. Operational Archives. Declassified. Gives exact location, time, and circumstances surrounding the torpedo attack on this British armed trawler. Ship specifications are given. Good source. [N.H.C.]

_____. "Summary of Statements of Survivors of the SS *Robert C. Tuttle*." n.d. Operational Archives. Declassified. Gives exact location, time, and circumstances surrounding the sinking of the tanker SS *Robert C. Tuttle*. Ship specifications are given. [N.H.C.]

_____. "Summary of Statements by Survivors of the SS *Santore*." n.d. Operational Archives. Declassified. Gives exact location, time, and circumstances surrounding the sinking of the ore steamship *Santore*. Ship specifications are given. [N.H.D.]

Navy Department. Office of the Deputy Chief of Naval Operations (Air). "Air Task Organization in the Atlantic Ocean Area." 1945. Guide No. 45. Navy Library. Declassified. Chronological report on the organization and operation of the air power in the Eastern Sea Frontier. Good details on those involved in antisubmarine warfare efforts. [N.H.C.]

Navy Department. Office of Naval Operations. "Report on the Interrogation of Survivors of U-701 Sunk by U.S. Army Attack Bomber No. 9-29-322, Unit 296 B.S. on July 7, 1942." n.d. Operational Archives. Declassified. Report contains interesting details from eyewitnesses. Also, reports on other U-boats. Note: interrogators did not discover from the crew that the U-701 was the ship responsible for laying mines off Virginia Beach. [N.H.C.]

Smith, Richard K., Lt. "An Inventory of U.S. Navy Airships with Miscellaneous Characteristics, Performances and Contract Data, 1916 — 1961." Individual personnel, n.d. Operational Archives. This report contains notes on the Navy's acquisition of airships during World War II. [N.H.C.]

U.S. Naval Administration in World War II. "BUORD Underwater Ordnance." Vol. 9, 1940. Guide No. 78. Navy Library. Declassified. Report describes the development, operation, and actual use of such underwater devices as mines and hedgehogs. [N.H.C.]

_____. "CINCLANTFLT, Commander in Chief. U.S. Atlantic Fleet." Vol. 1, 1946. Guide No. 138. Navy Library. Declassified. Report describes the development of the Atlantic Fleet. Details the campaign against the German U-boats. [N.H.C.]

World War II Command File. *Atik.* n.d. Operational Archives. Declassified. Detailed historical documents concerning the Q-ship *Atik.* Of particular interest are the copies of correspondence and replies between the Navy and an American mother who for years had to struggle to learn the truth about her son's fate following the destruction of the *Atik* while on a secret mission.

**Books**

Barksdale, Arthur Sydnor, Jr. History of the Norfolk Navy Yard in World War II. Portsmouth: Marshall Butt Library, 1945. Barksdale is a retired Navy Lieutenant Commander. His history of the base covers a wide variety of its features and functions during World War II. [Marshall Butt Library - Reserve Shelf]

Cremer, Peter. U-boat Commander. Annapolis: Naval Institute Press, 1984. First-hand account of U-boat warfare by former submarine commander Peter Cremer. Good insights into the effect of America's antisubmarine warfare. Good appendix listing, with details, the destruction of all German U-boats, including those that were scuttled. [Life-Saving Museum].

Doenitz, Karl. Memoirs: Ten Years and Twenty Days. Annapolis: Naval Institute Press, 1990. Grand Admiral Karl Doenitz gives his reflections on the German U-boat offensive during World War II. Contains detailed information on the implementation of operation Paukenschlag. Well-written with good maps. [D 781 .D613]

Flanders, Alan B. and Captain Arthur C. Johnson, Jr. Guardians of the Capes: History of Pilots and Piloting in Virginia Waters from 1611 to the Present. Lively, Virginia: Brandylane Publishers, 1991.

Morison, Samuel Eliot. <u>The History of U.S. Naval Operations in World War II</u>, vol. 1, <u>The Battle of the Atlantic, September 1939 — May 1943</u>. Boston: Little, Brown, and Company, 1947. Superbly written. Describes in detail a vast array of weapons and equipment used in antisubmarine warfare. Appendix lists areas mined by German U-boats. Names of U-boats listed. [D 773 .M6 V.1]

_____. <u>The History of U.S. Naval Operations in World War II</u>, vol. 10, <u>The Battle of the Atlantic Won, May 1943 — May 1945</u>. Boston: Little, Brown, and Company, 1956. Details antisubmarine warfare training on the East Coast. Describes sinking of U-521. Tells how U-566 successfully defended itself against U.S. air attack. Data on the organization of the Tenth Fleet. [P.P.L. Rot 940.540 Mo]

Nalty, Bernard C., Dennis L. Noble, and Truman R. Stobridge. "Wrecks, Rescues, and Investigations." <u>Scholarly Resources</u>, 1978. Virginia Beach Life-Saving Museum, Virginia Beach, Virginia. Contains copy of original Coast Guard report which gives details on coastal foot patrols. Brief account of how a man on patrol spotted German saboteurs coming ashore on the beach at Amagansett, Long Island. [Life- Saving Museum]

Nash, Harry. <u>Submarine Warfare in Local Waters, World War II</u>. n.d. Bound copy of newspaper articles in Portsmouth Library. Articles dealing with attacks on all types of ships in the Fifth Naval District waters by German U-boats. Includes articles on press conferences given by the Navy dealing with the submarine menace. All articles by Harry Nash. [P.P.L.]

Weinert, Richard P., and Colonel Robert Arthur. <u>Defenders of the Chesapeake — The Story of Fort Monroe</u>. Annapolis: Leeward Publications, 1978. Excellent source of information on the history of Fort Monroe. Good details on how Fort Monroe's defenses were prepared for wartime status. [P.C. of Frank Shield]

Werner, Herbert A. <u>Iron Coffins</u>. New York: Holt, Rinehart, and Winston, 1969. Herbert Werner served as a German U-boat captain during World War II. Excellent account of U-boat operations. Includes undocumented account of a mining operation conducted within sight of Norfolk, Virginia. However, Navy minesweeping records show that no mines were ever found. [D 780 .W45 1969]

## Miscellaneous Reports, Letters, Interviews, and Videocassettes

Clark, Harry. Interview, Chesapeake, Virginia. 14 October 1989. Retired Navy captain. First-hand account of the rigorous antisubmarine warfare training conducted in Key West Florida. Includes information on how one American submarine of World War I vintage was lost during training with only three survivors. [P.I.]

Commander Defense Area Group. "Report of Minesweeping Operations, 16 June 1942." Fifth Naval District Inshore Patrol Section Base. Confidential Report to Commander Eastern Sea Frontier, 9 July 1942. Virginia Beach Life Saving Museum, Virginia Beach, Virginia. This report details the mine sweeping operations conducted when a convoy struck the German mines laid off Virginia Beach. One of the enclosures is a chart showing where the vessels from the convoy struck a mine and/or went down. [Life-Saving Museum]

Commander in Chief. U.S. Atlantic Fleet. Office of Naval Intelligence. "Information on German U-boats No. 1." 1942. Report in possession of Frank Shield, Virginia Beach, Virginia. Compilation of post mortem reports on the sinkings of various German submarines. [P.C. of Frank Shield]

Degen, Horst, captain of the U-701. Letter from Luxembourg, Germany, to Mr. I.M. Punnett, and Mr. Anthony Hancox, in Birmingham, England. 14 November 1965. Copy in possession of author. Personal account by Horst Degen of how he and the crew of the U-701, which he commanded, deployed mines near the entrance of the Chesapeake Bay. This is a copy of his own typed letter. Contains his own drawings. His own penned notes are in the corners of the pages. [P.C. of authors]

_____. Interview by authors, 27 November 1991, Luneburg, Germany. Tape recording.

Fahey, John A., Navy airship Captain. Interview by authors, 4 November 1992, Norfolk, Virginia. Tape recording.

Fifth Naval District. Office of Naval Intelligence. "Sinking of German Submarine U-85, Report on the Disposition of Bodies and Effects." n.d. Copy of report in possession of Frank Shield, Virginia Beach, Virginia. This Navy report describes the sinking of the U-85 and the results of the examination of the dead crewmen who were in the water when depth charges detonated near them. [P.C. Frank Shield]

Hardegan, Reinhard, captain of U-123. Interview by authors, 28 November 1991, Bremen, Germany. Tape recording.

Hasler, Robert, Navy intelligence officer. Interview by authors, 5 November 1992, Norfolk, Virginia. Tape recording.

Hudgins, Linwood, U.S. Coast Guard Buoy Tender. Interview by authors, 11 January 1992, Portsmouth, Virginia. Tape recording.

Kane, Harry. U-701: A Real Life "Das Boot." n.d. Virginia Beach Life-Saving Museum, Virginia Beach, Virginia. Videocassette. Video presentation describing the mining off Virginia Beach by the U-701. Also includes a description of the sinking of the U-701 by an Army bomber, with comments by the pilot Harry Kane. [Life-Saving Museum]

Kelly, Joseph A., U.S. Coast Guard. Interview by authors, 13 October 1991, Norfolk, Virginia. Tape recording.

Powell, Stanley H., M.D. Interview by authors. Portsmouth, Virginia. 15 May 1990. A medical doctor's insights into the effects of a depth charge's concussion on a human body while in water. [P.I.]

Rathke, Helmut, captain of U-352. Interview by authors, 29 November 1991, Flensburg, Germany. Tape recording.

"Record of Proceedings of a Court of Inquiry Convened at the Naval Operating Base, Norfolk, Virginia, by order of the Secretary of the Navy to inquire into the loss of the H.M.S. *Ceylonite*, on or about June 15, 1942." 30 July 1942. Virginia Beach Life-Saving Museum, Virginia Beach, Virginia. Inquiry examines all of the pertinent facts surrounding the sinking of H.M.S. *Ceylonite* after it struck a German mine near the coast of Virginia Beach. It determined that this loss was an unavoidable casualty of war. [Life Saving Museum]

Swink, Frederick G., U.S. Coast Guard officer. Interview by authors, 8 August 1991, Norfolk, Virginia. Tape recording.

Tilton, Rollin L. "History of Chesapeake Bay Sector." Fort Monroe, Virginia, 1 March 1945. Copy in possession of Fielding L. Tyler. Declassified. Tilton was a brigadier general, U.S. Army, in command of the Chesapeake Bay Sector. Excellent first hand account of the administration and operation of the forts and other harbor defenses during World War II. Good maps and charts. Some mention of the Navy's cooperative role in these defenses. [P.C. of Fielding L. Tyler]

Truver, Dr. Scott C., ed. United States Naval Institute Professional Seminar. "ASW: The Navy's Top Warfighting Priority?" 27 February 1990. U.S. Navy seminar that discussed the current status of antisubmarine warfare. References were made to the lessons learned from the German U-boat offensive during World War II.

Tyler, Fielding L. "Fort Story, Virginia, World War II Armament Tour." Copy in possession of Fielding L. Tyler. A detailed history of Fort Story that contains a complete listing of all armament used in each of the batteries. Originally part of a tour package. [P.C. of Fielding Tyler]

_____. "Ships Attacked by U-boats in the Fifth Naval District During Operation Drumroll." Copy in possession of Fielding L. Tyler. Personal record compiled by local historian and retired Army Lieutenant Colonel Fielding L. Tyler. Lists all ships that he knows were sunk in the Fifth Naval District. [P.C. of Fielding Tyler]

## Articles and Newspapers

Belke, T.J. "Roll of Drums." USNI Proceedings, United States Naval Institute, April 1983. Brief but substantial Navy article on the devastation wrought by a handful of German U-boats off the East Coast during operation "Paukenschlag." [Journal V1.U8 109(4)]

Blackford, Frank. "When War Was At Our Doorstep." The Virginian-Pilot and The Ledger-Star, 17 October 1971. Detailed account of the first days of the German submarine menace off Virginia. Describes how unprepared the region was. The laying of mines off of Virginia Beach by the German submarine U-701 and the sinkings that followed are also described. [P.P.L. M.F.]

Bond, Sharon. "A Bit of England on Outer Banks." The Ledger Star, 27 December 1979. Article describes the burial site in North Carolina for several British sailors whose bodies washed up on shore following the sinking of their ship by a U-boat.

"Crowds at Virginia Beach Hear Sound of Explosions at Sea — Navy Withholds Information." Norfolk Virginian-Pilot, 16 June 1942. Brief description of Virginia Beach crowd reactions to the explosions caused by mines left by the U-701. Paper notes that the Navy failed to release any information on the incident. [ODU M.F.]

Galuska, Peter. "Huge Guns Watched the Bay When Nazi Push Was Feared." The Virginian-Pilot, 25 September 1977. Article gives a complete overview of the harbor defenses during World War II. Mentioned convoy that struck mines off Virginia Beach in June 1942. Interesting that it did not relate this to the mines laid by the U-701. Mentions Werner's book, Iron Coffins, which records a minelaying incident within the Bay in 1943.

"No Information on Explosions." The Portsmouth Star, 16 June 1942. Similar account to that in The Virginian-Pilot. Navy withheld information on explosions occurring off Virginia Beach. Source given as the Associated Press. [P.P.L. M.F.]

Offley, Ed. "Chesapeake Bay Mined — War Came Close to Home." The Virginian-Pilot and The Ledger-Star, 8 July 1982. Good recounting of the mining of the Chesapeake Bay by the U-701. Contains good diagrams. [P.P.L. M.F.]

_____. "Confrontation in the Atlantic — The Death of U-701." The Virginian-Pilot and The Ledger-Star, 9 July 1982. Fine recounting of the sinking of the U-701 by an Army bomber. Also tells how several members of the submarine's crew, including the Captain, Horst Degen, managed to survive. [P.P.L. M.F.]

_____. "Wartime Foes Reunite as Friends." The Virginian-Pilot and The Ledger-Star, 7 July 1982. Article describes the reunion of two wartime adversaries: German Submarine Captain Horst Degen and American Army Pilot Harry Kane. Degen's submarine, the U-701, was sunk by Kane in an Army A-29 medium attack bomber. [P.P.L. M.F.]

Pearson, Irene. "Sub Hits Two Merchantmen off the Coast, 46 Aboard Sunk Ship Reach Base — One Crewman is Killed." The Portsmouth Star, 17 June 1942. Details on ships sunk off Virginia Beach by mines laid by U-701. Like The Virginian-Pilot, it assumes the ships were torpedoed. Interesting note is that the paper acknowledged that they were in possession of details regarding the incident the day before. However, under a voluntary censorship agreement with the Navy, they withheld the information. [P.P.L. M.F.]

Py, Ray. "The Deep: Sub Wreckage Is Popular with Divers." The Virginian-Pilot and The Ledger-Star, 29 June 1986. Article describes how wrecks, such as the U-85, sunk off of Cape Hatteras, have become popular with sport divers. [P.P.L. M.F.]

Sanders, Harry. "King of the Oceans." USNI Proceedings, August 1974. Report by retired Vice Admiral Harry Sanders. Fleet Admiral Ernest J. King's achievements during World War II are chronicled in this Navy article. Author was a member of King's wartime staff. [Journal V1.U8 100(8)]

Sullivan, Frank. "Battle of Atlantic Pushes Virginia's Shores — Two
Merchant Ships Torpedoed Before Eyes of Thousands Who Line
Resort Front to See Grim War Drama." The Virginian-Pilot, 17
June 1942. Describes the reactions of the crowd at Virginia Beach
when a convoy struck mines laid by the U-701. Interesting
account of how and why they believed the ships were torpedoed.
Only a brief note suggesting that mines may have been involved.
Details sinkings and response by aircraft and Navy vessels that
dropped depth charges in the area. Details on those injured and
the one casualty. No follow-up to correct their assumption that
torpedoes were responsible for the sinkings. [ODU M.F.]

"Warfare Against Subs In Area Is Planned By Navy." The Portsmouth
Star, 19 June 1942. Overly brief report on antisubmarine
warfare in the Fifth Naval District. Includes comments from
Captain Russell S. Crenshaw, USN, who was just assigned at
that time to the Norfolk Naval Operating Base as assistant to the
Commandant. [P.P.L. M.F.]

## Secondary Sources

### Books

Ageton, Arthur A. The Naval Officer's Guide. New York: McGraw-
Hill, 1943. Reference book for information on Navy
organization and procedures during World War II. Contains charts
of the Navy districts. [Marshall W. Butt Library - Reserve Shelf]

Belker, C.D. K-Men. Odenburg: Gerhard Stalling Verlag, 1968.
Account of the German frogmen and midget submarines.
Illustrates the K-force, the organization responsible for creating
and operating the small sea weapons for the German Navy. In
America, it was feared such weapons could be used to infiltrate
the defenses of the Fifth Naval District. [D 781 .B4313 1973]

Blueprint for Survival: A Plan for the Development of Fort Wool.
Norfolk: Old Dominion University, 1976. Contains a short but
informative history of Fort Wool. [F 232 .F66 .B58]

Brennecke, Jochen. <u>The Hunters and the Hunted</u>. New York: W.W.
Norton & Company, 1957. Translated from German. A
chronological history of Germany's U-boat offensive against all
its enemies. Special section describes offensive off America's
East Coast. [D 781 .B713]

Buchheim, Lothar-Gunther. <u>U-Boat War</u>. New York: Alfred A. Knopf,
1978. Translated from German. Although it does not report in
detail the attack on America's East Coast, it does vividly describe
the experiences of life aboard a U-boat. Staggering array of
photographs taken by German submariners that show every
aspect of the grueling life aboard a U-boat. [D 781 .B7813 1978]

Cope, Harley Francis. <u>Serpent of the Seas</u>. New York and London:
Funk & Wagnalls Company, 1942. An overview of America's
level of readiness during the early days of World War II.
[V 210 .C66]

Cox, Albert W. <u>Sonar and Underwater Sound</u>. Massachusetts:
Lexington Books, 1974. Explains the types of sonar devices used
in antisubmarine warfare, particularly during World War II.
Presented is a brief history of the major sonar developments in
antisubmarine warfare from 1916 to 1974. [VM 480 .C64]

Cross, Wilbur. <u>Challengers of the Deep</u>. New York: W. Sloane
Associates, 1959. Account of how different countries pursued
the development of submarines. Several chapters illustrate how
Germany and America developed submarines for use during the
world wars. [v 210 .C75]

Crowther, James Gerald. <u>Science at War</u>. New York: Philosophical
Library, 1948. Overview of the value of science in warfare.
Description of the development of radar, highlighting the
achievements of such men as Sir Robert Alexander Watson-Watt.
Last section describes scientific developments in naval warfare
such as sonar. [UG 145 .C7 1948]

Farago, Ladislas. <u>The Tenth Fleet</u>. New York: Ivan Obolensky, 1962.
Interesting details on the creation of the Tenth Fleet, "the fleet
without a ship." Chronicles how unprepared the East Coast was

during the first days of the U-boat offensive. Describes how improvements were made. [Dx783 .F3]

Frank, Wolfgang. <u>The Sea Wolves</u>. New York: Rinehart & Company, 1955. German account of the U-boat offensive against the American East Coast. Description of the struggle by Grand Admiral Karl Doenitz to get more ships and men from Adolf Hitler. Illustrates how the Allies gained partial control over the U-boats through scientific developments, more efficient operational techniques, and increased production of cargo ships. [D 781 .F742]

Gannon, Michael. <u>Operation Drumbeat</u>. New York: Harper & Row, 1990. Depiction of the German U-boat offensive called <u>Paukenschlag</u> or Operation DRUMBEAT. Gannon centers his vivid text on the war cruises of the U-123 commanded by Reinhard Hardegen, who made two devastating voyages to America's East Coast, sinking 19 cargo ships. The book is well documented and researched. Gannon used both American and German sources extensively. His in-depth interviews with Reinhard Hardegan, who now lives in Bremen, Germany, plus other crew members of the U-123, add extraordinary detail, delivering a view of the war from the enemy's perspective. In addition, Gannon reviews the severity of the American Navy's poor defense of the East Coast and how it was slow to respond even after the threat became real. [Virginia Beach Public Library, 940.5451 G1980]

Gray, Edwyn. <u>The Devil's Device</u>. London: Seeley, Service and Company, 1975. Story about Robert Whitehead who invented the torpedo driven by compressed gas. This invention by the British scientist twice nearly defeated his own country. Weapon is described as the dominant weapon at sea for over half a century. Photographs of the early torpedoes. First successful demonstration in 1870. [V 855 .W5 .G7 1975].

Hartmann, Gregory K. <u>Weapons That Wait</u>. Annapolis: United States Naval Institute, 1979. Review of mine warfare in the United States from the Civil War to the present. Details of mines used in World War II such as those deployed in the Fifth Naval

District.  Appendix A gives a chronological listing of the technological events relevant to the development of mine warfare.  [V 856.5 .U5 .H3 1979]

Hezlet, Arthur Richard, Sir.  <u>The Submarine and Sea Power</u>.  London: Peter Davies, 1967.  Evolution of the submarine as a ship of war is described from its infancy to the present day, with conjectures towards the future.  Chapter eight gives a lengthy description of the German U-boat's role in the battle of the Atlantic.  [V 857 .H48]

Hickham, Homer J., Jr.  <u>Torpedo Junction</u>.  Annapolis:  Naval Institute Press, 1989.  Current book on antisubmarine warfare operations in the Fifth Naval District during World War II.  The book centers on the action off North Carolina.  Good details, particularly of the operations by several Coast Guard vessels.  [Life Saving Museum]

Horton, Edward.  <u>The Illustrated History of the Submarine</u>.  New York: Doubleday, 1974.  Brief report on the development of submarines.  Several chapters describe their use during the world wars.  Excellent photographs.  [V210 .H64]

Horton, Joseph Warren.  <u>Fundamentals of Sonar</u>.  Annapolis:  United States Naval Institute, 1959.  Technical description of the use of sonar.  Of particular interest is the description of naturally occurring sound waves found in the sea, such as those produced by marine life, which gave trouble to many sonar operators during World War II.  [VK 388 .H7 1959]

Hoyt, Edwin P.  <u>The Death of the U-boats</u>.  New York:  McGraw Hill, 1988.  Overview of the German U-boat offensive throughout the war.  Details given on Italian submarines.  Details also given on the development and success of escort groups.  Description of German developments in U-boat technology.  Included is a rare diagram of a German "schnorkel" [snorkel] that explains its operation.  [D 781 .H678 1988]

_____.  <u>The U-boat Wars</u>.  New York:  Arbor House.  1984.  Details the organization and operation of Germany's U-boat fleet.

Details Grand Admiral Doenitz. Section on the offensive against America entitled "Doenitz's War Against America."
[D 781 . H688 1984]

_____. U-boats Offshore. New York: Stein and Day, 1978. Brief description of the antisubmarine operations conducted off America's East Coast. Information presented in a series of vignettes. Noticeable omissions though, such as description of the sinking of the U-701 that fails to mention its role in the mining off Virginia Beach. [D 781 .H69]

Hughes, Terry, and John Costello. The Battle of the Atlantic. New York: The Dial Press, 1977. Overview of the Battle of the Atlantic. Charts giving battle statistics. Section on convoy tactics and equipment used. Excellent photographs.
[D 770 .H83 1977]

James, Geoffrey P. Defeat of the Wolf Packs. Novato: Presidio Press, 1986. Centers on the submarine warfare from 1943 to 1944. A review of the entire conflict is given. The lives of the U-boat crews are also described. Excellent photographs. Glossary for use as a reference for terms relevant to antisubmarine warfare.
[D 781 .J67 1986]

Keatts, Henry, and George Farr. Dive Into History: U-boats. New York: American Merchant Marine Museum Press, 1986. Brief but informative description of the following German submarines: UC-97, U-85, U-352, U-701, U-853, and U-2513. Appendix lists status of the crews for all the U-boats. Another reference list gives all the known German ranks and their United States equivalent. Excellent photographs. [P.C. of Frank Shields]

Kuenne, Robert E. The Attack Submarine — A Study in Strategy. New Haven: Yale University Press, 1965. Book resulting from the General Economics Systems Project at Princeton University, which strove to further the study of large-scale decision models and to increase their application to the analysis of real-world problems. Addresses the problems in deploying submarines. Relates analysis of problems surrounding the use of submarines during World War II. Presents details on both American and

German submarine offensives. Includes map of the Battle of the Atlantic. Appendix lists all the major warships sunk by submarines during World War II. [V 210 .K8]

Lenton, H.T. American Gunboats and Minesweepers. New York: Arco Publishing, 1974. Detailed photographs. Lists all the auxiliary vessels of the United States Navy during World War II. Illustrates that when the war began few escort ships were available. Consequently, a wide assortment of vessels were used including converted fishing boats, large yachts, ex-British Corvettes, and some of the "Eagle" boats built by Henry Ford during the First World War. All these ships are described in the text. All played a vital role as antisubmarine vessels. [V 880 .L47]

_____. German Submarines. 2 vols. New York: Doubleday & Company, 1965 & 66. Complete listing of all types of German submarines used during World War II. Includes all pertinent statistics, diagrams, and occasional photographs of the U-boats. [V 859 .G3 .L4 1966 Vols. 1 & 2]

Lott, Arnold S. Most Dangerous Sea — A History of Mine Warfare, and an Account of U.S. Navy Mine Warfare Operations in World War II and Korea. Annapolis: U.S. Naval Institute, 1959. History of the U.S. Navy's minelayers and minesweepers in World War II. Pertinent information on mine operations in the Fifth Naval District. Appendix listing those U.S. ships destroyed by "friendly" mines. [D 773 .L6]

Low, Archibald Montgomery. The Submarine at War. New York: Sheridan House, 1942. Published in 1942, this book offers an excellent look at how the Allies viewed submarines both offensively and defensively during the early days of World War II. The antisubmarine measures of the day are examined well. The arming of convoy ships is discussed. In addition, the use of Q-ships, heavily armed converted cargo ships disguised as harmless merchant ships, is advocated. [V 210 .L6 1942]

Macintyre, Donald. The Battle of the Atlantic. New York: The Macmillan Company, 1981. Descriptions of the convoy system and the early efforts by the Germans off the East Coast. Appendix describing the weapons used in the battle of the Atlantic. However, this appendix is far from complete. [D 770 .M2]

_____. U-boat Killer. Annapolis: Naval Institute Press, 1956. Detailed account of the role played by the destroyer in America's antisubmarine warfare effort. Depicts life aboard destroyers. It also illustrates the role played by destroyers in hunter-killer groups. [D 780 .M32 1976]

Middleton, Drew. Submarine, the Ultimate Weapon: Its Past, Present, and Future. Chicago: Playboy Press, 1976. Although not a formal history of the development of submarine warfare, chapter four gives an account of the Germans' reasoning behind the use of submarine warfare. Tonnage of shipping sunk by the Axis given. [V 210 .M52]

Price, Alfred. Aircraft Versus Submarine. London: William Kimber, 1973. Although told from the British perspective, the development of aircraft as an effective antisubmarine weapon is described herein. Developments by both England and America are highlighted. Text gives details on such developments as high frequency centrimetric wavelength radar used on such aircraft as the B-24 Liberators. Also, description of the developments in weapons from mines and bombs to the powerful rockets that proved so lethal to the submarines. Details on the various ways depth charges were used. [V 214 .P68]

Rouse, Parke, Jr. Roll Chesapeake Roll. Chesapeake: The Norfolk County Historical Society of Chesapeake, 1972. History of the Chesapeake Bay. Chapter 11 deals with the sinking of the German submarine U-85. Good photos. [F 187 .C5 .R 68]

Taylor, Theodore. Fire on the Beaches. New York: W.W. Norton & Company, 1958. Interesting account of the battle of the Atlantic. Information on antisubmarine warfare. Chapters such as "Operation Paukenschlag" and "East Coast" provide good data on the East Coast's poor defensive capability and the German plans to exploit them. Good information on the rescue operations performed by blimps. [D 780 .T 3]

Tsipis, Kosta. <u>Tactical and Strategic Antisubmarine Warfare</u>.
Cambridge: MIT Press, 1974. British monograph that describes
in detail the many aspects of antisubmarine warfare. Coverage
of such pertinent areas as underwater acoustics, detection
systems, tactical antisubmarine warfare, antistrategic submarine
warfare, and antisubmarine warfare and strategic liability.
Appendices listing the various antisubmarine warfare systems
that have been devised and their countries. [V 214 .T78 1974]

Watson-Watt, Robert Alexander. <u>The Pulse of Radar</u>. New York: Dial
Press, 1959. Detailed account of the development of radar and
its military applications. Details the contributions radar made in
the Allied war effort. Highlights of such systems as the "Huff
Duff," which used an instantaneous visual direction finder. An
autobiography. The author, a British scientist, was instrumental
in many of the developments in radar. [UG 610. W28]

Westwood, David. <u>Anatomy of the Ship - The Type VII U-boat</u>.
Annapolis: Naval Institute Press, 1984. Elaborate, technical data
on the different production varieties of the Type VII U-boat.
Schematics of each version of the Type VII U-boat constructed.
Descriptions of armament included. Good photos. [P.C. of Frank
Shield]

Wheeler, Major William Reginald. <u>The Road to Victory - A History of
Hampton Roads Port of Embarkation in World War II</u>. 2 vols.
New Haven: Yale University Press, 1946. Pertinent data on the
amount of material transported through Hampton Roads during
World War II. Highlights the vital importance of the area to the
war effort. The second volume gives data on how and where
prisoners of war were interned in the area during the war. Good
photos. [810 .T8 .W5 V.1 & V.2]

Willoughby, Malcolm F. <u>The U.S. Coast Guard in World War II</u>.
Annapolis: United States Naval Institute, 1957. Details the Coast
Guard's cooperative work under the Navy during World War II.
Description of the security efforts for the ports. Appendix C
gives a summary of the notable Coast Guard escort operations in
the Atlantic. [D 770 .W456]

Zim, Herbert Spenser. <u>Submarines — The Story of Undersea Boats</u>. New York: Harcourt, Brace and Company, 1942. Published in 1942, this book offers a view of the antisubmarine weapons and tactics at that time. In chapter 18, the book explains the development and use of such devices as nets, mines, depth charges, sonar, convoys, and aircraft. Schematics describe such things as the triggering mechanism for a magnetic mine. [VM 365 .Z5]

## Articles

Chewning, Alphus J. "Buried on Foreign Soil." <u>Virginia Cavalcade</u>, Autumn 1989. Short but interesting overview of antisubmarine warfare in local waters. Primarily centers on the sinking of the U-85 by the USS *Roper*. Also contains relevant details on the sinking of the steamer *City of New York*. A baby was born in one of the lifeboats from this ship. [F 221. V74]

Hickam, Homer H., Jr. "Day of Anger, Day of Pride — The <u>Icarus</u> Encounters the U-352." <u>American History Illustrated</u>, January 1983. Vivid account of the sinking of the German submarine U-352 by the U.S. Coast Guard Cutter *Icarus*. Description of the *Icarus* and crew. Details of the attack. [Life-Saving Museum]

Syrett, David. "The Battle of the Atlantic." <u>The American Neptune</u>, Winter 1985. Detailed account of the battle of the Atlantic. Describes America's poor level of preparedness for the German U-boat offensive. Information on a variety of aspects of why the battle of the Atlantic turned in favor of the Allies in 1943. Covers such pertinent features as technological innovations, intelligence operations, the use of convoys, and the efficiency, or inefficiency, of military commands. [V1. A4]

## Encyclopedias

Academic American Encyclopedia. S.v. "Submarine," by John F.
    Guilmartin, Jr. Description of submarine development and
    implementation. Overview of German U-boats produced during
    World Wars I and II. Describes development of antisubmarine
    weapons, vessels, and tactics. [REF AE 5 .A23 1988 V.18]

Collier Encyclopedia. 1988 ed. S.v. "Submarine," by John D. Alden.
    Illustrates the development of submarine technology. Highlights
    German developments during World War II, such as the snorkel,
    which enabled submarines to remain submerged while using their
    diesel engines. [REF AE 5 .C 6834 1988 V.21]

The Encyclopedia Americana. 1985. S.v. "Submarine," by Edward
    Stafford. Depicts the living conditions within a World War II
    submarine. Subsection entitled "Antisubmarine Warfare"
    describes the development of tactics and weapons from World
    War I to the present. Describes sonar's role in World War II.
    [REF AE 5 .E333 1985 V.25]

Great Soviet Encyclopedia. S.v. "Antisubmarine Aviation." Describes
    the development and use of aircraft to destroy submarines
    during World War II. [REF AE 5 .B58 V.21]

_____. S.v. "Antisubmarine Defense." Description of how a wide
    variety of military measures must be used in conjunction with
    each other to create an effective submarine defense.
    [REF AE 5 .B58 V.21]

_____. S.v. "Antisubmarine Nets." Brief description of the design
    and deployment of antisubmarine nets. [REF AE 5 .B58 V.23]

_____. S.v. "Antisubmarine Ships." Describes the development
    of ships with the specific role of detecting and destroying
    submarines. Illustrates American and British developments
    during World War II. [REF AE 5 .B58 V.21]

_____. S.v. "Depth Charges." Short but cogent illustration of the
    variety of depth charges used during World War II.

[REF AE 5 .B58 V.6]

The New Encyclopedia Britannica. 1987 ed. S.v. "Submarine." Short
but detailed description of the development of submarines,
particularly during World War II. [REF AE 5 .B58 V.6]

_____. S.v. "War, The Technology of War." Detailed report on the
German submarine developments during World War I and II.
Good subsection entitled "Antisubmarine Measures."
Information on the use of mines, cruisers, and destroyers.
[REF AE .E363 1987 V.29]

# Index

Henke, Werner  4
*Herbert Jacob Jones*, MV (*DD-130*)  45
High Frequency Direction Finder (Huff-Duff)  109
Hitler, Adolf  1,11,113
Horne, F.J.  43
Howe, Captain H.W.  52,53
Hudgins, Captain Linwood  8,9,10,27,28,29,31,34,91,92

# I

*Icarus*, USCG  54,55,71,72
Inshore Patrol  63

# J

*J.A. Mowinckel*, MV  125
*Jackson*, USCG 26
*Jacob Jones (DD61)*  45
Jester, Lieutenant Maurice P.  54
Joint Operations Center  32,64,66

# K

K-Class airships  102
K-gun  108
Kane, Second Lieutenant Harry J.  55,56,57,62
*Kassandra Louloudis*, SS  118
*Kassos*, MV  74
Kelly, Joseph  37,38,39,40,41,42,89
Key West  35,45,46,47,48,52,104
"Killer Team Doctrine"  108
King, Admiral Ernest J.  8,13,24,25,32,42
*Kingston Ceylonite*, HMS  19,124

# L

*Lady Hawkins*, SS  115
*Lancing*, SS  121
Langley Field  7,96,101
Leahy, Commandant  27
Leary, Robert F.  24
Leonard, Edwin M.  44
Le Breten, David M.  24
*Liberator*, SS  119
*Libertad*, SS  126
*Liebre*, SS  120
Little Creek, VA  30,36,37,38,40,41,46,47,65,70

*Ljubica Matkovic*, SS  124

# M

MAD (magnetic airborne detector)  48,103,106
*Malchace*, SS  121
*Malay*, SS  115
*Manuela*, SS  124
*Marore*, SS  117
*Menominee*, SS  120
*Mercury Sun*, MV  119
*Mississippi*, USS  28
*Monitor*, USS  75
*Monte Mulhacen*, SS  74
Morehead City, NC  10,46,75
"mousetrap"  109
*Muldanger*, SS  22,124

# N

Naval Operating Base  2,6,31,32,35,53,64,78
Newport News Shipbuilding  31,96
*Nighthawk (CGR-2008)*  37, 41
Nimitz, Admiral Chester  8
*Nordal*, SS  124
Norfolk Naval Shipyard  2,5,31,96
Nunally, Joe  40

# O

*Oakmar*, SS  119
*Ocean Venture*, SS  116
Ocracoke, NC  34,38,40,46
Old Point Comfort  31,98
*Olean*, SS  117
*Olinda*, SS  117
Operating Defense Plan  96
Operational Intelligence Unit  67,68,75,77
Operation Drumbeat  1,11,12,111
Operation *Paukenschlag*  12,111,113
Operation Torch  15
*Orchid*, USS  8,9,10,30,31,92
Oregon Inlet  29
*Otho*, SS  121

# T

# U

# V

# W

# Y

# ABOUT THE AUTHORS

**James R. Powell (Russ)** is a native Virginian who has always been fascinated with local history. His father, Dr. Stanley H. Powell, was also a history buff who shared numerous fascinating stories of local history. This had a profound impact in the educational choices Russ would make. He completed his undergraduate work at Emory & Henry College, where he studied mass communications and history, then pursued his graduate studies at Old Dominion University (ODU), where he received his Masters in History in 1991. He is currently employed by Portsmouth Public Schools where he has functioned as a department head and as a social studies teacher.

**Alan B. Flanders**, a Portsmouth, Virginia native, has written numerous articles and books on Virginia's maritime history. His columns on Hampton Roads have regularly appeared in the *Virginian-Pilot* of Norfolk, Virginia for the last twenty-one years. He currently teaches at Old Dominion University and holds a B.A. M.A. and Ph.D. in history. Flanders is also a Fellow by Special Election at St. Edmund Hall, Oxford University.